IRISH ARCHITECTURAL AND DECORATIVE STUDIES
Volume XX, 2017

IRISH ARCHITECTURAL AND DECORATIVE STUDIES

THE JOURNAL OF THE IRISH GEORGIAN SOCIETY – VOLUME XX, 2017

IRISH ARCHITECTURAL AND
DECORATIVE STUDIES
The Journal of the Irish Georgian Society
Volume XX, 2017

Published by the Irish Georgian Society
© Irish Georgian Society and the authors, 2017
All rights reserved.

ISBN 978-1-910140-19-2

This annual journal continues the publishing tradition
of the Irish Georgian Society's *Bulletin*
(38 volumes, 1958-1997).

Edited by Finola O'Kane

Produced for the Irish Georgian Society by Gandon
Editions
design   John O'Regan (© Gandon, 2017)
production   Nicola Dearey
printing   Nicholson Bass, Belfast
distribution   Gandon and its overseas agents

GANDON EDITIONS
Oysterhaven, Kinsale, Co Cork
T +353 (0)21-4770830 / E gandon@eircom.net
W www.gandon-editions.com

The Irish Georgian Society gratefully acknowledges the
grant-aiding of this book by:
OFFICE OF PUBLIC WORKS
CASTLETOWN FOUNDATION
Mr JIM THOMPSON
and a private donor

cover
Detail of the chimneypiece and wallpaper in the Red
Drawing Room at Castletown
(photo: Will Pryce; courtesy COUNTRY LIFE Picture Library)

frontispiece
The Obelisk near Castletown, 140 feet high
(engraving of the Conolly Folly (1740)
from the Noble and Keenan map of Kildare, 1752)

THE IRISH GEORGIAN SOCIETY

The Irish Georgian Society aims to encourage an
interest in and the preservation of distinguished
examples of architecture and the allied arts in Ireland.
Further information – and membership application
details – may be obtained from:

THE IRISH GEORGIAN SOCIETY
City Assembly House, 58 South William St, Dublin 2
T +353 (0)1-6798675 / E info@igs.ie
W www.igs.ie

IRISH ARCHITECTURAL AND DECORATIVE STUDIES

THE JOURNAL OF THE IRISH GEORGIAN SOCIETY – VOLUME XX, 2017
EDITOR: FINOLA O'KANE

———

Foreword

SIR DAVID DAVIES

T HIS HANDSOME VOLUME OF THE IRISH GEORGIAN SOCIETY JOURNAL IS DEDICATED
to Castletown, and marks the fiftieth year of its rescue by Desmond Guinness
and its opening to the public. Our editor, Finola O'Kane, introduces its contents
more fully elsewhere in the volume. I congratulate her on the difficult task of pulling
together such an interesting themed issue, and thank the Castletown Foundation and the
Office of Public Works for working with us on this volume.

It seems extraordinary that this is the twentieth volume of this series, which was
launched in 1998 when a decision was made to expand the old and much loved *Bulletin*.
At the time Desmond Guinness explained its extended remit: 'The new manifestation
of the *Bulletin* acknowledges the importance of the entire spectrum of Ireland's post-
medieval architecture and its special need for protection, interpretation, understanding
and appreciation.' Some years later, the Knight of Glin articulated the centrality of this
journal to the IGS: 'The scrupulous scholarship that this journal promotes permeates
and informs all our activities.' I thank the series of editors who have maintained the
scholarly rigour of the Journal for two decades – Seán O'Reilly, Nicola Figgis, William
Laffan and Conor Lucey – and also its distinguished editorial board who oversee it.
Thank you, too, to our publishers Gandon Editions who have been responsible for the
design and production of each of the twenty volumes published so far – in itself quite
an achievement.

The Journal has been fortunate in attracting sponsorship, and we are grateful to
the generosity over the years of the Apollo Foundation, the Ireland Funds, the Mark
Fitch Fund, the Esmé Mitchell Trust and the School of Irish Studies Foundation. For
many years we received generous support from the J. Paul Getty Jr Charitable Trust and
the estate of the late Paul Mellon. We thank Jim Thompson for his generosity, as well
as a supporter in the United States who has helped fund the Journal in recent years, and
who wishes to remain anonymous.

This year marks one of the great highlights of the Irish Georgian Society's history – the restoration of the City Assembly House – the first, purpose-built public art

gallery in either Britain and Ireland, and possibly in Europe – and the wonderful exhibition that opens in June, honouring the Society of Artists who built it in the mid-1760s. The exhibition includes some eighty paintings by artists who exhibited with the Society, including great names of eighteenth-century Irish art such as Robert Carver, Robert Healy and Hugh Douglas Hamilton. Many of the exhibits were first exhibited in this great octagonal exhibition room 250 years ago, for example Thomas Roberts' bravura *Frost Piece*, exhibited in William Street in 1769, or William Ashford's masterly *View of Gibraltar*, included in the 1775 exhibition. The exhibition has been made possible through the work of its curator, Dr Ruth Kenny, who worked with William Laffan in tracing works for the show, and a steering committee led by Dr David Fleming. It has been realised through the generosity of the public and private lenders and those who have donated funds to ensure its success. *Exhibiting Art in Georgian Ireland: the Society of Artists' exhibitions recreated* will open in the great Exhibition Room – newly dedicated to the Knight of Glin whose vision and persistence has contributed so much to the success of the exhibition. We remember the Knight and also pay tribute to our distinguished founders Desmond and Mariga Guinness for their years of work that has taken the IGS from a tea party in Carton sixty years ago to the dynamic organisation it is today. I hope this will be further demonstrated in September when we launch a major exhibition of the work of the contemporary artist John Nankivell who has produced the most extraordinary body of work exploring the Irish country house and related buildings. This exhibition has been made possible through the great generosity of one of our American benefactors.

———

William Ashford (1746-1824) A View of Gibraltar

1775, oil on canvas, 50.5 x 92 cm (detail) (private collection)

This painting was one of the original exhibits of the Society of Artists exhibition which is being returned to the Exhibition Room where it was first put on public display. It was included in the 1775 exhibition and was singled out for praise in the review by the critic for the Hibernian Journal: 'Though Gibraltar is but a barren rock, no other than a fertile hand could lay before us so good a portrait of it'.

Editorial

FINOLA O'KANE

FOR MANY IRISH PEOPLE, CASTLETOWN HOUSE DEFINES THE IRISH EIGHTEENTH-century country house and demesne. It also conveys the complexities of Irish conservation and the role that the Irish Georgian Society has played in that history. This twentieth volume of *Irish Architectural and Decorative Studies* commemorates the fiftieth anniversary of Desmond Guinness's purchase of Castletown and his subsequent donation of the house, together with a substantial portion of its demesne, to the Irish nation for current and future generations.

The man who built Castletown, William 'Speaker' Conolly, was extraordinarily successful in the buccaneering environment of early eighteenth-century Ireland. Followed by his wife Katherine Conolly, his grand-nephew William Conolly II and then by the well-known Louisa Conolly and her husband Tom, this period has tended to be the most appreciated and the most reiterated. After its heyday in the eighteenth century, Castletown soldiered on through the nineteenth century, escaping a proposed transformation into a barracks in 1808 and enjoying a relatively sedate and conservative period of country-house pursuits until the early decades of the twentieth century. Thanks to the efforts of Desmond Guinness and friends, the Irish Georgian Society, the Castletown Foundation and more recently, the Office of Public Works, Castletown remains a great Irish country house.

This volume aims to broaden our understanding of Castletown House and the political, cultural and social contexts that created it. Castletown's social history is documented to an exceptional degree for an eighteenth-century Irish estate, thanks to Desmond Guinness's and Lena Boylan's skip-hunting efforts. It has tried to address, where possible, areas where less research has taken place, in particular the early and late periods of Castletown's history and the lives and interests of the less familiar characters. It also pushes beyond the physical boundaries of Castletown's reach towards the Wonderful Barn and Dublin's city centre. We have also tried to include the varied viewpoints of art and architectural historians, architects, archaeologists, curators, conservators and historians. Kyle Leyden's essay explores the strategic agendas behind Ireland's early eighteenth-century architecture while Neil Crimmins reminds us that there was a Castletown before the Conollys and that the Dongan family, in losing their estates in both Kildare and New York, invested in a block of land on James's Street in Dublin. Patrick Walsh's essay brings William Conolly II, the Speaker's grand-nephew, out of obscurity while Patricia McCarthy describes Tom Conolly's equine pursuits with care and enthusiasm. The wider Castletown, suggesting the estate's influence far beyond the demesne wall, is explored by Cóilín Ó Drisceoil in his essay on the planting and farming history of the corkscrew Wonderful Barn.

Aidan O'Boyle revisits the history of Castletown's art collections, now being assiduously reassembled or sympathetically suggested by the Castletown Foundation and the OPW. Christopher Moore reveals the painstaking work involved in restoring just one aspect of Castletown's layered history in his essay on the conservation of the silk wallhangings of the Red Drawing Room by the Castletown Foundation, a project that commemorates the life and work of our distinguished past president Kevin B. Nowlan. The complex past and ongoing work of Castletown house and demesne's conservation and restoration by the Office of Public Works is told by Dorothea Depner. Our past editor, Nicola Figgis explores the auction of Ann Conolly's collection at Christies in 1797 and Jeanne Meldon writes on the lost Castletown demesne portraits that were sold at that sale to a Mr. Ewan. Would that Castletown had them still.

This volume is also dedicated to the architectural, literary and landscape historian Rolf Loeber (1942-2017), who made an outstanding contribution to Irish scholarship through his many publications. From his early and seminal 1973 essay 'Irish Country Houses and Castles of the late Caroline Period: an unremembered past recaptured' published in *The Bulletin of the Irish Georgian Society* and *A Bibliographical Dictionary of Irish Architects* (1981), to the groundbreaking *A Guide to Irish Fiction 1650-1900* (2006, co-authored with Magda Stouthamer-Loeber and Anne Burnham) and, more recently, as co-editor of *Architecture 1600-2000*, volume IV of *Art and Architecture of Ireland* (2014), Rolf's publications have helped generations of Irish historians, architects and engineers to understand this country's environment. That he accomplished this while continuing to work as a distinguished professor of psychology speaks of a truly humane cast of mind, one shared by his wife, co-author and distinguished scholar Magda. An advocate and practitioner of interdisciplinary research, well before it was dreamt of, Rolf always brought the acute sensibility of an intrigued and critical visitor to bear on innumerable aspects of this country. Always a Dutchman, emigré not in Ireland but in Pittsburgh, Pennsylvania, his sympathetic yet detached point of view will be greatly missed. He supported the Irish Georgian Society from its early years, living with Magda in Castletown House in 1972-73, where they helped Desmond Guinness to begin the long conservation journey that this journal aims to document. *Ní fheicimid beo ar a leithéid arís*.

———

AUTHORS' BIOGRAPHIES

NEIL CRIMMINS is an architect working in Dublin.

DOROTHEA DEPNER has a PhD from TCD, where she worked as a visiting research fellow until 2015. She co-edited, with Guy Woodward, *Irish Culture and Wartime Europe, 1938-1948* (Four Courts Press, 2015). She currently works in National Historic Properties at the OPW.

NICOLA FIGGIS is head of the UCD School of Art History & Cultural Policy. She was co-author with Brendan Rooney of *Irish Paintings in the National Gallery of Ireland* (Dublin, 2002) and principal author and editor of *Art and Architecture of Ireland, Volume 2: Painting 1600-1900* (RIA / Yale, 2014).

KYLE LEYDEN is a AHRC-CHASE PhD candidate at the Courtauld Institute of Art completing his thesis '"The Epitome of the Kingdom": the politics of fine building and the fashioning of Irish national identity 1719-1782'. He is currently working as a research consultant with the Courtauld Connects project.

PATRICIA MCCARTHY was awarded a PhD by TCD. As an architectural historian she has published widely on eighteenth and early nineteenth-century topics. Her most recent book is *Life in the Country House in Georgian Ireland* (Yale, 2016).

CHRISTOPHER MOORE has been a member of the Castletown Foundation since 2000 and was chairman from 2013 to 2018.

JEANNE MELDON is a town planner with a particular interest in conservation and landscape. She has served on several national and European advisory bodies, is a member of the Irish Architectural Archive and co-chair of the Castletown Foundation.

AIDAN O'BOYLE completed his PhD thesis on 'The assembly, display and dispersal of art collections in Ireland 1750-1950' at Trinity College Dublin in 2011. He is currently working as a freelance art historian.

CÓILÍN Ó DRISCEOIL is lead archaeologist for the archaeological project at Barn Hall. He is managing director of Kilkenny Archaeology consultants. He co-edited, with the late John Bradley and Michael Potterton, *William Marshal and Ireland* (Four Courts Press, 2017).

PATRICK WALSH teaches eighteenth-century Irish history at TCD. He is author of *The Making of the Irish Protestant Ascendancy: the life of William Conolly, 1662-1729* (Boydell Press, 2010) and, with Anthony Malcomson, *The Conolly Archive* (Irish Manuscripts Commission, 2010). He is a director of the Castletown Foundation.

———

Irish Georgian Society

———

BENEFACTORS AND SPONSORS 2017

The Irish Georgian Society is very grateful to its supporters in the United States who provided generous assistance to our projects in 2017 through their donations and participation in fundraising events.

PLATINUM BENEFACTOR
($50,000+)
Gilbert Butler Foundation
Elizabeth Dater Jennings
Kay and Fred Krehbiel
Denise and Thomas Tormey
John and Nellie Tormey Trust

GOLD BENEFACTOR
($20,000 – $49,999)
The Crowe Family
Jane and Thomas Kearns
Annette Lester

SILVER BENEFACTOR ($10,000
– $19,999)
Susan and Coleman Burke
Thomas W. Dower
    Foundation
Mary K. Hartigan
Silvia and Jay Krehbiel
OWL Foundation
Heather and John Picerne
Eleanor and John Sullivan
Marti and Austin Sullivan

BENEFACTOR
($5,000 – $9,999)
Annabelle and Denis
    Coleman
Alexandra and Thomas
    Cooney
Mary Lynn Cooney
Ellen G. FitzSimons
Terry and Wesley Guylay
Nancy Gorman

Jessica Lagrange
Suzy Moran
Bonnie O'Boyle
Chip and M.A. Quinn
Pam and Scott Schafler
Niall Smith
Michael H. Steinhardt
Catherine and Lee Styslinger
Julia and Hans Utsch

PATRON ($2,500–$4,999)
E. Garrett Bewkes
Michael and Debra Blute
Cindy and Christopher Galvin
Janie and Gene Goodwillie
Maribeth Heeran
Nancy and Paul Keeler
Patrick Killian
Lynn and John McAtee
Dorothea and Bruce Nawara
Lyssa Piette and Dorothy
    Pattishall
Diana Revson Charitable
    Trust
Sarah and Sean Reynolds
Regina and George Rich
Maria and George Roach
Lawrie and Edward Weed

SPONSOR ($1,000–$2,499)
Robert Bartlett, Jr.
Friederike Biggs
Charles M. Brennan
Thomas P. Connor
Thomas Coyle
Bridget and James Flanagan

Gillian Fuller
Jerome L. Greene
    Foundation
Marie and James Hayes
Pepper and Michael Jackson
Diane and Jeffrey Jennings
Delia Roche Kelly
Trudy and Michael Kelly
Michael Kovner and Jean
    Doyen de Montaillou
John Lance
Cherilyn Lawrence
Live Oak Foundation
Peter Clayton Mark
Priscilla Martin
Robert J. Morrissey
Rose Marie O'Neill
Chantal O'Sullivan
Imelda and Andras Petery
Kathleen and James Poole
Maureen Elizabeth Sheehan
    Charitable Fund
Denise and Harold Smith
Maureen and Edward Smith
Steinberg Family Foundation
Sherri Stephenson
Dyanne Connelly Tosi
Nancy and Glen Traylor
John Vaile
Maribeth Welsh and Ellen
    Welsh
Brian White and James
    Kinney
Elizabeth Yntema and Mark
    Ferguson
William Lee Younger, Jr.

Irish Georgian Society

―――――――

PATRON MEMBERS AND SUPPORTERS 2017

BENEFACTOR MEMBERS

Michael and Gianni Alen-Buckley
John E. Carroll
Sir Charles Colthurst
Sir David Davies
Mary Hobart
Michael Roden

CORPORATE SUPPORTERS

Devenish Properties
Irish Life
Merrion Property Group
O'Mahony Pike Architects Ltd

PATRON MEMBERS

Galen Bales
Michael Boyle
Glenn Bradshaw
Sindy Broe
Sir Francis Brooke
Mr & Mrs G.H. Browne
Rev Fr Gabriel Burke
Maura Byrne
Shane and Emma Cahill
Dr Marjorie Carney
Francis Carr
Edmund Corrigan
Ailbhe and Frank Cunningham
V.E. Dillon and Hon. Mrs Dillon
Guy Everington
Bruce Finch

Trevor FitzHerbert
John and Deirdre Flynn
Dr Brendan Glass
Nancy C. Gorman
Frederick Hennessy
Gabriel Hogan
Neill Hughes
Raymond Hurley and Victoria Browne
Brian Kingham
Anthony L. Leonard
Dermot and Camilla McAleese
Susannah McAleese
Ivor McElveen
Peter MacNamara
Paul Martin
Michael and Gemma Maughan
Michael J. Meagher
Patrick Murray
John J. O'Connell Architects Ltd
Gay O'Neill and Robin Hall
Andrew and Delyth Parkes
Bill and Celeste Phelan
Ian and Enda Quinn
C.W. Raper
Mary Reade and Seamus Hogan
K.C. Rohan
The Earl and Countess of Rosse
Mairin Schwarz
Kevin Shannon
David Sheehan
June A. Stuart
Jim Thompson
Ronald Wood

CORPORATE PATRONS

Taylor Architects
Declan Costello
Principal Construction
    Services Ltd
Mike Jones
Úna Ní Mhearáin
Punch Consulting Engineers

SUPPORTER MEMBERS

Tom Aherne and family
Stephen Alexander
R.P. Blakiston Houston
Mary Bowe
David Britton and Karen
    Reihill
Robert Burke
Daniel Calley
Anthea Cameron
Rev Peter Campion
Brian Clerkin
Damian Collins
Jane Coman
Geoffrey Cope
Thomas Cosby
Brian Coyle
Rose Mary Craig
Robert Cummins and family
Ewan Currie and family
Gerard Daly and family
Martin and Bernadette
    De Porres Wright
Anne Dillon Carrigan

Patrick Dowling
Conor and Mareta Doyle
Mr Phelan Doyle
Dr Thomas Duncan
Emerald Stained Glass
L. Feeney and family
Garrett Fennell
John FitzGerald
Patrick Gageby
Seán and Philomena Hagan
John and Leela Hardy
Richard J. Hawkes
Yvonne and John Healy
Adam Hernes
Kevin Hurley
The Earl of Iveagh
John P. Joyce
Patrick Kelleher and family
Aidan Kelly
Marie Kennedy
Tom and Caitriona Kiernan
Gregory Kronsten and family
Renee Lawless
Dr Emer Lawlor
John P Lyons and family
Conor McCoole
Fionn MacCumhaill
James Paul McDonnell
Peter J. McElwee
Christine MacGiffin
Dr. Jane McManus
Eileen Magner-Smith
Eamonn Marrett
Lindsay Montgomery
Gerard and Fiona Moore and
    family

Charles B. Morris
Logan Morse
Frank Newman
Bryan O'Brien
Eugene O'Connor
Rev Stephen W. Rea
Fiona Reilly and Tarquin
    Blake
Lady Heather Robinson
Breeda Rochford
James Sammon
Bernard Segrave-Daly
Nicholas Sheaff
Geraldine Shepherd and Lt.
    Col. John H. Shepherd
Marcus and Irene Sweeney
Rev Michael Thompson
John Tierney
Brendan and Valerie Twomey
Peter Verity
Nuala Walker and Richard
    Kenny
Michael Wall
Brian Walsh and Barry
    Doocey
Wendy Whelan
Barney White-Spunner
Gavan Howard Woods and
    Jennifer Hickey
Thomas Woulfe
Johanna Woulfe-Hyland

———

Substance over style: Castletown and the protean politics of Irish 'improvement'

KYLE LEYDEN

W HEN COMPARED WITH THEIR COUNTERPARTS IN BRITAIN, IRISH BUILDINGS constructed during the first half of the eighteenth century have received little academic scrutiny. The perennially beguiling narrative of the primacy of Castletown within the corpus of Irish architectural history – secured through a combination of its supposed architectural novelty, the importance of its patron and his progeny, and, most vitally, the compellingly dramatic story of its later reinvention as the headquarters of the Irish Georgian Society in 1968 – has meant that it has received rather more attention than most.[1] Yet, despite being arguably the most closely scrutinised Irish building of the eighteenth century, recent work has suggested that many fundamental questions remain about its conception, its meaning and its true place in the narrative of Irish architectural history.[2] In the past, commentators have tended to concentrate almost exclusively on the identification of its architect and/or its influence on the development of the form and 'style' of the Irish country house type.[3] In doing so, there has been a general tendency to cast the Castletown project as *sui generis*, a watershed in the conceptualisation of Irish country-house construction and design which had no domestic precedent and which marked a deliberate, conspicuous and definitive architectural and philosophical break with all that had been built before.[4] As a result, writers have struggled to find an imported stylistic model for Castletown, from Palladio's Veneto through the great Renaissance *palazzi* of Rome to the work of Burlington and his circle in England. None could be found which satisfactorily encompassed the full range of unique architectural solecisms which characterise the house, and, indeed, the majority of country houses built in Ireland before 1750.[5]

The task of defining Castletown's architectural style had, it seemed, been made particularly difficult by the tantalising lack of contemporary evidence left by William

1 – Entrance hall, Castletown (photo: Will Pryce; courtesy COUNTRY LIFE Picture Library)

Conolly (1662-1729) and his circle as to the stylistic sources they consulted or emulated. Much may be gleaned from the well-known correspondence between George Berkeley (1685-1753) and John Perceval, 1st Earl of Egmont (1683-1748), as to the patriotic motivations behind many of the deliberate decisions made regarding the architect, scale, plan and appearance of the house.[6] 'You will do well', Perceval stated to Berkeley,

> to recommend to [Conolly] the making use of all the marbles he can get of the production of Ireland for his chimneys, for since this house will be the finest Ireland ever saw, and by your description fit for a Prince, I wou'd have it as it were the Epitome of the Kingdom, and all the natural Rarities she affords should have a place there. I wou'd examine the several woods there for inlaying my floors and wainscote with our own Oak and Walnut: my stone stairs should be of black palmers stone, & my buffet adorned with the choicest shells our strands afford. I would even carry my zeal to things of art; my hangings, beds, cabinets & other furniture shou'd be Irish & the very silver that ornamented my locks & grates shou'd be the produce of our own mines.[7]

However, having been so enthusiastically outspoken on these minutiæ, neither Berkeley nor Perceval offered any opinion as to the appropriate architectural 'style' which should be adopted, nor do they refer to any existing architectural model outside Ireland which should be emulated. Indeed, William King (1650-1729) actively advised against the importation of foreign models for Irish country houses, a practice which, he argued, had led to the adoption of what he described as 'inconveniencys'.[8]

In the context of this silence on 'style' or 'model', later writers have generally ascribed discrepancies between any chosen model and Castletown to provincial licentiousness, misunderstanding of European precedent or the *retardataire* tendencies of provincial architects.[9] More recent re-evaluations of architectural classicism, particularly in the work of Barbara Arciszewska and Peter Burke, do not view classicism as a fixed and immutable concept, and instead explore each building within its unique historic, socio-political, geographic and economic context in order to demonstrate that different regions negotiated the language of classicism in order to mediate often contrasting meanings in different ways during different periods.[10] In particular, there has been a growing recognition of what Burke describes as a conscious process of 'hybridization' of classical with native or seemingly anachronistic architectural forms, often to communicate potent messages about the contemporary socio-political context of the building project.[11]

Few considered the highly persuasive value of contemporary silence on 'style', for therein can arguably be found the strongest possible evidence that contemporary viewers simply did not view Castletown within this paradigm. To contemporary viewers, the value and meaning of Castletown was not found by using a visual checklist of appropriate stylistic features that could place it comfortably within the confines of a particular architectural style or related it to an appropriate emulated architectural model. Instead, its importance and message were to be communicated through the adoption of a uniquely

Irish and, most importantly, rational architectural form which would, through its plan, form, function and economy, encapsulate the very essence of an increasingly prosperous, peaceful and politically independent Irish state.

In considering the inherent 'Irishness' of the architectural fruits of these labours, Alistair Rowan has concluded that 'it is hard to discern anything that is specifically Irish' about eighteenth-century Irish country houses.[12] This reflected a general tendency among later commentators to read a narrative of stylistic 'other'ness and colonial possession into all the forms of classicism that developed in eighteenth-century Ireland and to cast all Irish country houses as monuments of a hegemonic attempt to put the relative dominance of the English state on display, thus ignoring the specific mediation and reception of buildings constructed in the period prior to 1750.[13] The definition of architectural 'Irishness' was once again limited to a checklist of architectural features (such as the 'decorative taste' at Castletown or the 'quirk of planning' in the upstairs lobby of Bellamont Forest, county Cavan, which were unique to Ireland and that do not appear on buildings elsewhere. It is only by severing the definition of 'Irishness' from this stylistic architectural paradigm and instead encompassing the complex socio-political and cultural context, which, it will be argued, was consciously mediated through architecture in eighteenth-century Ireland, that the true value and 'Irishness' of Irish eighteenth-century architecture can be ascertained.

In taking Castletown out of this 'stylistic' paradigm, its true significance within an ongoing and protean discourse on Irish 'improvement' can be appreciated. Recent studies on Early Modern attitudes to national self-awareness have stressed the centrality of the concept of 'improvement' to the self-fashioning and promotion of the nation state as being distinct from its neighbours, rivals or colonial motherland.[14] Originally a concept signifying no more than the profitable cultivation of land, in the seventeenth century the term 'improvement' became synonymous with a host of measures aimed at national civic perfection.[15] Critical to the concept was the material progress of the State, but 'improvement' encompassed much more than financial gain; economic growth was merely the means by which a series of moral and socio-political aims could be achieved and empirically measured, including the advancement of manufactures and international trade, the eradication of poverty, the education of the populace, and the promotion of distinct national self-awareness and joint enterprise among the citizenry.[16]

Paul Slack has argued that in seventeenth-century England, 'improvement became a fundamental part of the national culture, governing how the English saw themselves'.[17] Slack has stressed the central importance of economic progress to the concept of English 'improvement', suggesting that the principal character of that kingdom, as distinct from its European neighbours, was found in its mercantile prowess.[18] In Ireland, the discourse surrounding 'improvement' was similarly focused upon the prosperity of the kingdom, secured though increased overseas trade. From an Irish perspective, however, this trade was in turn reliant on the fruits of good native land stewardship, agricultural reform, the development of Irish manufactures, and the benevolent, independent government which

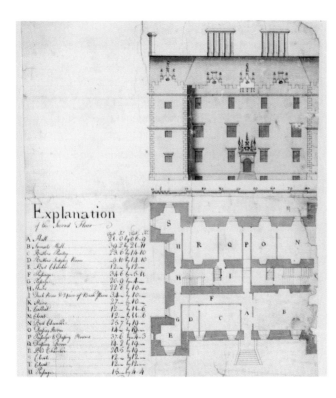

2 – *Portumna Castle, county*
Galway: elevation of the north
front and plan of the second
(principal) floor

This undated drawing shows the
development of an axial spinal space
dividing parallel suites of rooms with
paired staircases serving either end
of the house. (courtesy Royal Irish
Academy © RIA)

opposite

3 – *Gabriel Beranger,*
RATHFARNHAM CASTLE
1774, pencil and watercolour
(courtesy National Library of
Ireland)

would secure all of these.[19] Irish 'improvement' thus encompassed much more than merely mercantile prosperity.

The establishment of a vibrant class of resident Irish landlords was long recognised as the *sine qua non* of Irish 'improvement'.[20] Writing in 1738, Samuel Madden argued that English absentee landlords had 'used Ireland just as the Spaniards do the Indians and the vast Savannahs of America', thereby laying waste to 'one of the finest countries in the Kingdom'.[21] He therefore extolled Irish landlords to 'build on [their] Estates and encourage [their] tenants to do so'.[22] He declared that these landlords should build in a style which 'not only beautified the face of our country but [gave] heart and life and spirit to our people'.[23] The crucial role of country house architecture within the project of Irish 'improvement' was thus threefold: firstly, it acted as redemptive economic stimulus through the practical processes of construction; secondly, it encouraged the permanent settlement of resident landlords whose financial interests would depend upon Ireland's prosperity; and thirdly, it had a powerful communicative role as a cultural object which would visually assert the increasing self-confidence and independence of the Irish state.

Evidence of the Protestant élite's wish to improve the prosperity of Ireland though the encouragement of permanent familial settlement arguably stretches back to the building projects of Adam Loftus (1533-1605) at Rathfarnham (1583) and Richard de Burgh, 4th Earl of Clanricarde (1572-1635), at Portumna (*c*.1618) (Plates 2, 3). These early

attempts at 'improvement' had concentrated upon reducing the primarily defensive nature of most Irish domestic architecture, thus increasing the desirability of an Irish estate as a permanent residence rather than as a distant asset or defensive bolt-hole. By importing English plans and appearances for these houses, the builders of seventeenth-century Ireland sought to invite favourable comparisons with the relative peace and civility of England.[24] In the 1673 *Present State of Ireland*, the unnamed author stated that the Irish looked with great envy upon the English and 'their goodly houses ... [and] at the improvements they made of their Estates'.[25] Like many other writers, the anonymous author applauds Ireland's larger towns for displaying evidence of English custom through their fine buildings, civic government and manners. Dublin, in past years a 'mean and inconsiderable metropolis', is much extolled as bearing 'in some parts somewhat a like resemblance with that of the City of London'.[26] Similar views were expressed by John Dunton, who in 1699 described Drogheda as 'a handsom, cleane English-like town and the best I have seen in Ireland'.[27] These texts connect respectability, Protestantism and architectural development in a way which conflates the concept of 'Englishness' with a universal project of 'civilisation', and it is arguable that these writers considered the term 'English' not so much as connoting a state of nationality as a state of civility.

In *The Present State of Ireland*, the improvement of English landholdings in Ireland was encouraged on the very practical basis that 'by enjoying such plentiful Estates in that Realm, [the English] will thereby be better enabled be to breed up a sufficient number of learned Protestant Lawyers and Divines to serve the Publick which will very much tend to the strengthening of the Civil Government of that Kingdom'.[28]

It is, however, clear that this idea of 'improvement' being derived from English 'civility' was not one which was apparent during the construction of Castletown from 1719. No contemporary writer on the Castletown project invited or proposed any comparison, positive or otherwise, with England. Something had clearly changed in the way 'improvement' was conceptualised.

To understand how the concept of Irish 'improvement' altered over the course of the seventeenth century, it is necessary to consider how Irish attitudes changed towards 'English civility'. Toby Barnard has argued that there was an incremental sense of disenchantment with England during this period, which he characterises as 'a personal journey made by numerous ... settlers from England, Wales and Scotland' as they increasingly realised that their interests, as a unified body, were not necessarily co-existent with those of England.[29] Barnard traces this journey through the critical change in tone across the writings of one such settler, Richard Lawrence. Lawrence had arrived in Ireland as a colonel in Cromwell's army in 1649 and died there in 1684, having established his principal financial and family interests in the kingdom.[30] In *The Interest of England in the Irish Transplantation* (1655) and *England's Great Interest in the Well Planting of Ireland with English People* (1656), the 'Anglicisation' of Ireland through the establishment of plantation settlements along the south-east coast was declared to be in the joint interests of the English living in Ireland and of the colonial motherland, which, by 'the inlargement of the English nation so near itself, would add much to its strength, riches and reputation, much more than the West Indian Plantations'.[31] Through use of this colonial paradigm, it seems clear that Lawrence considered himself, as a settler, thoroughly allied to the English interest. By 1682, however, he had performed something of a *volte face*, penning a stinging critique of English governance in Ireland which he squarely blamed for the abject poverty of the nation, suggesting that in the interests of financial prosperity Ireland should be governed by Irishmen alone.[32] This opinion may well have been coloured by Lawrence's own abortive attempts to establish himself in Irish manufacture, which were largely thwarted by protectionist English trade legislation.[33] This arguably reflects a critical moment in the narrative of Protestant Irish national self-awareness, when the settler population began to think of itself as a unified body engaged in joint enterprise, certainly distinct from the English, and – perhaps – even Irish.

It can be argued that by the time of the publication of William Molyneux's polemic *The Case of Ireland being Bound by Act of Parliament in England* in 1698, such attitudes had crystallised. The context of the work was a sustained campaign on the part of the English legislature to impose restrictions on the trade of Irish woollens which would have crippled the Irish economy and devastated the estates of many settlers who had established their principal financial interests there.[34] Molyneux's polemic set out the historical, legislative and legal basis for Irish legislative independence. He considered the nature of the English presence in Ireland and concluded that the assumption of the Lordship of Ireland by Henry II had not been in the manner of a conquest but rather a voluntary submission by the governors, civil and ecclesiastical, of Ireland to the Crown of England, which left the separate legislative apparatus of the kingdom intact under the shared Crown.[35] The proposed trade restrictions were thus cast as a usurpation both of Royal Prerogative and the inviolable independence of the Irish legislature.[36] Most tellingly, however, he argued that even if the assumption was to be considered a just conquest, the aggressor 'gets no Power over those who conquered with him; they fought on his Side, whether as private Soldiers or Commanders, but cannot suffer by the Conquest, but must at least be as much Freemen as they were before.'[37] Thus, only the 'ancient race of the Irish' could have suffered under any conquest by Henry II: 'the English and Britains who came over with him retain'd al the Freedoms and Immunities of Freeborn Subjects; they nor their Descendants could not in reason lose these'.[38] Molyneux asserted that it was

> manifest that the great body of the present People of Ireland are the Proginy of the English and Britains that from time to time have come over into this Kingdom; and there remains but a meer handful of the Ancient Irish at this Day; I may say, not one in a Thousand.

Leaving aside the paradoxical nature of the claim that Ireland was not conquered, but that nonetheless the majority of the population was now composed of the progeny of those who had come over from Britain, it is clear that the Protestant élite had shifted their self-identification from imported bringers of English civility to the very epitome of the Irish nation. No laws, Molyneux argued, could be imposed on these new Irish 'by any Authority of the Parliament of England but by the *Consent* and *Allowance* of the *People of Ireland*' as the civil and ecclesiastical state were settled there '*Regiæ Sublimitatis Authoritate*, solely by the King's Authority and their own good wills'.[39]

Lawrence and Molyneux thus seem to prefigure a period when 'Englishness' in Ireland connoted not 'civility' but rather the hostile mercantile competitor and the usurper of Irish legislative autonomy. This gradual but definitive shift in thinking is clearly reflected in the writings of those directly associated or concerned with the Castletown project. In his scathing attack on the absolutist government of Denmark penned in 1692, Robert, 1st Viscount Molesworth (1656-1725) wrote that London was the 'Epitom of the world' where visitors could learn 'Christian Liberty as well as other Christian Vertues', whereas he described Ireland as his '*pis aller*' in which he would 'perfectly degenerate'.[40] By 1712, however, George Berkeley was moved to write that 'London ... seems to exceed Dublin not so much in the stateliness or beauty of its buildings as in extent.'[41] By 1723, William King (1650-1729) declared London to be, in fact, 'the exemplar and fountain of most of the Luxury, vices and villainies that infect these kingdoms'.[42] He extolled Irishmen not to seek to emulate the great metropolis but instead to concentrate on domestic social improvement through the encouragement of 'fine building' and sound estate management, concepts which he suggested were lacking in England where the concept of 'improvement', centred on material progress alone, had been inevitably corrupted into a state of luxury, indulgence, moral degradation and vice.[43] By 1722, just as Conolly commenced the construction of Castletown, Robert Molesworth, who had suggested the services of Alessandro Galilei three years previously, recanted his previous opinions. In a letter to his brother John, he exclaimed, 'you must not despise an Irish Estate. I was once such a fool to do so ... but I have found ye folly of doing so, & find it to be ye sheet Anchor of ye family.'[44]

The promotion of the resident landlord with his family seat and principal financial interests situated in Ireland remained as central to the eighteenth-century Protestant conceptualisation of 'improvement' as it had done in the previous century. What had changed by 1722 was the means by which the Irish Protestant élite believed that improvement was to be achieved, from the importation of English modes of 'civility' to the patriotic defence of Irish economic and legislative independence.

The timing of Castletown's commencement in 1722 was no mere coincidence. The combined effect of a reduced native threat in the wake of the Treaty of Limerick, the increase in national production brought about by peace following the death of Louis XIV in 1715, and the decline of French militarism and the threat of invasion all made permanent settlement in Ireland a more attractive prospect. Most importantly, however, a growing appreciation among the Protestant population of Ireland, both Whig and Tory, that their landholdings (many of which had been confiscated from Jacobite sympathisers) could only be secured through a pragmatic acceptance of the realpolitik of the Hanoverian Succession meant that by the early 1720s, conditions in Ireland were sufficiently settled for a sustained and prodigious period of country-house construction. As William King reported to James Standhope in November 1715,

> this Kingdom is in perfect peace, for which we have great reason to thank God, the Papists continue very quiet and seem not by anything that appears to be in any disposition to give it disturbance ... As to the Protestants, they are generally <u>unanimous</u> in their zeal for His Majestie.[45]

The substantial demise of the Jacobite interest in Dublin following the purge of the Tory administration and flight of the Duke of Ormonde to the Court of the Pretender in 1715 meant that powerful positions were taken away from many Tory landlords, whose main financial and land interests were situated in England, and given to those whose fortunes had been made in the seventeenth-century settlements and who lived and worked on their Irish estates. These men were precisely those whose interest was best served by a flourishing Irish economy and an independent Irish legislature. Primary among these was Conolly himself.

Thus, in addition to the seventeenth-century desire to encourage familial settlement in Ireland, the archetypal Irish country house became, in the wake of growing disenchantment with the English political and financial interest in Ireland, a potent means of asserting the economic and political independence of the Irish state. This point gained a new urgency following the stinging legislative and judicial humiliation of the Irish parliament by the Declaratory Act of 1719. This Act declared the judicial and legislative supremacy of the parliament of Great Britain over that in Dublin, and must have come as a personal slight to Conolly.[46] It was a critical part of the Irish patriotic project of improvement that the building endeavours of Irish 'patriots' should answer this political challenge by promoting Ireland not as an obdurate subordinate satellite or, indeed, colony of England, but rather as an independent state among the states of Europe.[47] A comparison with England, positive or otherwise, was arguably thus irrelevant. That Irish country houses had to be as grand if not grander than anything seen in contemporary England could be attributed to a defensive colonial mind-set.[48] However, it is important to note the complete lack of any contemporary comparison being made between Castletown and comparable English houses during its construction. Those who contributed to the contemporary discourse on what form Castletown should take were not seeking an 'English', 'anti-English' or even 'Palladian' style. What they sought was a rational Irish architecture which would promote the patriotic project of improvement. This was pivotal to the legitimacy of their governance of Ireland as an independent state among the states of Europe.

The plan for Castletown, though rather implausibly said to be 'chiefly of Mr Conolly's invention', was the product of a species of 'committee of taste' which embraced the architectural opinions of a wide circle of architects, academics, politicians, social reformers and clerics that included Robert and John Molesworth, Edward Lovett Pearce, George Berkeley, Sir John Perceval and Alessandro Galilei.[49] What united this disparate group and arguably motivated Conolly to commence construction was a shared belief in the crucial part the building of Castletown could play in the socio-economic and political discourse surrounding the concept of 'improvement'. They were also united in that each had an association with Anthony Ashley-Cooper, third Earl of Shaftesbury (1671-1713).[50] Shaftesbury's influential *Letter Concerning the Art or Science of Design* firmly asserted architecture's place in mediating, securing and propagating the social, political, religious and economic benefits gained through the Glorious Revolution.[51] Shaftesbury's close association with those advising Conolly during the construction of Castletown, in particular Robert Molesworth whom Shaftesbury described as his 'Oracle in publick affairs ... a through Confident in ... private', meant that his thinking must have provided a convenient framework for their conceptualisation of the long-established project of Irish 'improvement' which was distinctly au courant.[52]

A reading of Shaftesbury's *Letter* reveals many correspondences between his thinking and the protean Irish concept of 'improvement'. Shaftesbury called for a 'national style' of architecture in England which would express the fruits of the Glorious Revolution and the English Constitution whilst providing economic stimulus to the country, mirroring the communicative and redemptive aims of Irish improvement.[53] Echoing the growing clamour against the inefficient and corrupt Office of the Surveyor General in Ireland, he criticised the political appointment of one Court architect (in his case Wren; in Ireland Burgh) under whom 'we have patiently seen the noblest publick buildings perish'.[54] The most striking parallel with the contemporary conception of the Castletown project can be drawn with his assertion that

> Even those Pieces too are brought under the common Censure, which, tho rais'd by private Men, are of such a Grandure and Magnificence, as to become National Ornaments. The ordinary Man may build his Cottage, or the plain Gentleman his country house according to his fancys: but when a great Man builds, he will find little Quarter from the Publick, if instead of a beautiful Pile, he raises at a vast expense, such a false and counterfeit Piece of Magnificence, as can be justly arraign'd for its Deformity by so many knowing Men in Art, and by the whole People, who, in such a conjecture, readily follow their opinion.[55]

This assertion that the 'great man' owes a patriotic responsibility not to merely build 'according to his fancys' but rather to further the patriotic development of his country is one which was absolutely critical to the Castletown project.

The most striking, and to many writers, frustrating aspect of Shaftesbury's *Letter* is its omission of any description of or model for what this new 'national architecture' would look like. Just as Perceval's letter to Berkeley fails to offer any guidance or model for the appearance of Castletown, so too does Shaftesbury leave the question of appearance and 'style' entirely unconsidered. Later writers on English architecture have tended to read Shaftesbury's letter into a teleological stylistic narrative in which 'Palladianism' inevitably displaced 'artisan mannerism' and the 'Baroque'.[56] Many later writers concluded that Shaftesbury offered little more than platitudes, and thus it inevitably fell to Burlington, Campbell and Kent to give architectural shape to Shaftesbury's philosophical tropes.[57] This singularly ignores the context in which Shaftesbury was writing, and fails to recognise that during this period, several architectural discourses – ranging from the stylistic pluralism of Hawksmoor's historicism seen particularly in his work at the University of Oxford, on the one hand, to the doctrinaire découpage of precisely copied pattern book precedents seen in the works of Burlington and his circle on the other, all set against the background of a growing interest in antiquarianism and a changing conceptualisation of history itself – were being promoted in England and Ireland, with no one being more likely than the others to dominate the form architecture would take.[58] It also leads to a tendency among later historians to overstate the novelty of the new 'style' in which commonalities with the displaced style must be circumvented or ignored. There is arguably a much more satisfactory explanation as to why Shaftesbury and Perceval do not describe in any detail the features of the 'national style' they espoused: they themselves were unsure what this new national architecture would look like, precisely because the precepts upon which it was to be based were not a checklist of architectural features but rather a discourse between architecture, politics and philosophy in which architecture, whatever its form may be, would display and promote the 'Genius of Liberty [and] the same Laws and Government, by which his Property, and the Rewards of his Pains and Industry are secur'd to him and to his Generation after him'.[59] This represents a much more nuanced definition of 'national style' than any stylistic visual checklist, and could, conceivably, include commonalities with the positive aspects of existing architecture both from within Ireland and copied from foreign precedent.[60] In this, Shaftesbury's architectural desiderata were precisely the same as those expressed by Irish builders. As Shaftesbury wrote of England,

> As her Constitution has grown, and been establish'd, she has in proportion fitted herself for other Improvements. There has been no Anticipation in the Case. And in this surely she must be esteemed wise, as well as happy; that ere she attempted to raise herself any other Taste or Relish, she secur'd herself a right one in Government. She has now the advantage of beginning in other Matters, on a new foot. She has her Models yet to seek, her Scale and Standard to form, with deliberation and good choice.[61]

The significance of the role of Shaftesbury's *Letter* in influencing the development of English architecture has come under significant academic scrutiny in recent years, with Alexander Echlin and William Kelley arguing that it was merely one philosophical discourse among many which sought to reform British architecture in the first years of the eighteenth century.[62] They argue that this discourse was displaced by the thinking of Burlington and had died out, along with the majority of its apologists, by 1726 without ever having formed the philosophical basis of a single building project.[63] What they perhaps failed to consider was the significant role of Shaftesbury's thinking in Ireland. Given Shaftesbury's unusually close relationship with Robert Molesworth, combined with the correlations between Shaftesbury's thinking and the ongoing Irish project of 'improvement', it seems more than arguable that the philosophical cross-pollination led to physical architectural results in Ireland.[64]

The influence of Shaftesbury in Ireland has been given significant consideration in the work of Edward McParland. As early as 1991 he argued that Robert Molesworth and his 'new Junta for architecture', composed of John Molesworth, Alessandro Galilei, Sir George Markham and Sir Thomas Hewett, were the true architectural successors of Shaftesbury – not Burlington – and that they had imported his thinking into Ireland through their professional and familial networks there.[65] It is not a very significant extension of this thinking to suggest that this influence continued in Ireland after 1726 when it is argued it ceased to exercise influence in England. Once Shaftesbury is severed from the orthodox development of 'English Palladianism', it is a small step to argue that the distinctive 'un-Englishness' of Irish country house architecture prior to 1750 is the result of the adoption and adaption of Shaftesbury's philosophy into a protean Irish project of improvement which succeeded in reforming Irish architecture in a way it had failed to do in England.[66] This argument appears to be greatly bolstered if one considers Shaftesbury's argument that his aims could substantially be promoted through two major building proj-

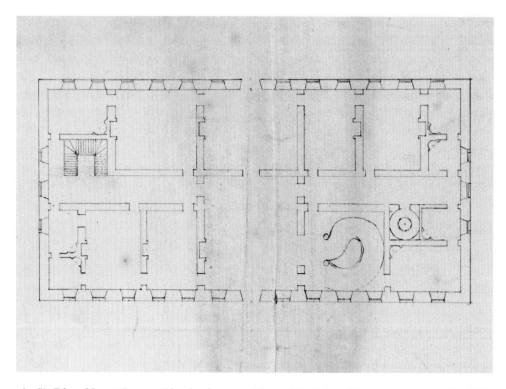

4 – Sir Edward Lovett Pearce, 'Plan for the ground floor of Castletown House as constructed', c.1720
This plan is not exactly as built; see page 73 for a later, more detailed plan.
(© Victoria and Albert Museum, Proby Collection, Vanburgh album E.2124: 165-1992)

ects which he declared to be the 'noblest subjects for Architecture; our Prince's *Palace* and our *House of Parliament*'.[67] If, like many contemporary commentators, one considers Castletown as a 'palace' for Ireland's 'chief governor', both projects had been commenced in Ireland before the end of the 1720s, whilst neither would be achieved in England until over a century later.[68]

So, what is the significance of this recognition of Castletown's place in an ongoing and protean project of patriotic improvement? Primarily, a departure from a 'stylistic' paradigm allows Castletown to be viewed not as something completely *sui generis*, but rather a development reflecting subtle and not so subtle changes in an ongoing discourse on Irish improvement. Many writers have attempted to encompass Castletown within the stylistic category of 'Palladian' through efforts to relate its plan and appearance to what has been deemed 'English Palladianism' or directly to models taken from Palladio's *Quattro Libri*.[69] The primacy of Castletown as 'Ireland's first "Palladian" house' has widely entered common currency. However, this approach has failed to adequately explain seemingly anachronistic references to existing Irish architecture or the 'English Baroque' in its plan and appearance.

In this respect, the axial corridor connecting two secondary servants' staircases is of particular note (Plate 4). A marked and very rational departure from the Palladian villa model with its interlinked rooms, this corridor allowed free circulation throughout the house without the occupant of any particular room being disturbed. In Ireland, there is evidence of the development of this practical plan as early as the first years of the seventeenth century. At Portumna Castle, county Galway, commenced at some point before 1618, the double-pile main block is planned with two suites of principal rooms arranged horizontally in parallel at each level, separated by a central space with a staircase at each end serving the two ends of the house (Plate 2). Whilst it has not yet developed into the practical axial corridor of Castletown (rather than being connected by a corridor, the staircases are separated by two service rooms and a bisecting corridor connecting front hall to the rear suite of rooms), it is a very small developmental step from the plan of Portumna to the practical rationality of Castletown. Tellingly though, whilst the committee was clearly open to the practical rationality of an axial corridor, the appearance of an enfilade of state rooms terminated by an antechamber at each end and including in their number a state bedroom along with a great hall on the ground floor, in addition to the presence at first-floor level of a long gallery, seem rather more *retardataire*, and undo much of the practical purpose of the axial corridor.

The traditional function of a great hall as a gathering space for an aristocratic household may have been obsolete as early as 1600, but its presence in a great many grand houses after this date was an essential status symbol confirming the builder's seigneurial status.[70] Its distinctly 'anti-Palladian' presence at Castletown, where Conolly was keen to assert his social and political status to his detractors, is thus entirely rational.[71] Furthermore, in offering seigneurial hospitality to his neighbours and tenants in the hall, Conolly had positioned himself as the archetypal benevolent resident landlord central to the project of Irish 'improvement'. The hall at Castletown is the only surviving major internal space to retain the entirety of its original decorative scheme (Plate 1). Fortuitously, it was always intended to be one of the most important interiors in the house, being a semi-public space. At first-floor level, columns and pilasters which at first glance appear to be of the Corinthian order are actually crowned with baskets of flowers, fruit and foliage in place of capitals (Plate 5). This may seem an entirely theatrical addition which completely defies 'Palladian' categorisation, but it is one which stressed the fruits of good land stewardship through reference to hospitality, abundance and plenty. Indeed, in making a conscious and deliberate decision to eschew the employment of the Corinthian Order where its use is prescribed in favour of an almost naturalistic 'anti-architecture', it is arguable that Conolly and the architectural committee were communicating a very specific message about the source of their architectural vocabulary. The Corinthian Order was described in Fréart's *Parallel* as 'the highest degree of perfection to which *Architecture* did ever aspire', and it is described with specific reference to the Callimachus myth and a rather fanciful engraving representing his invention of the order after observing a votive basket of fruits and flowers laid upon acanthus leaves (Plate 6).[72] Fréart's tract, along with Marc-Antoine Laugier's *Essai sur l'Architecture*, which had promoted

5 – Pillar at first-floor level of entrance hall,
Castletown, showing capitals composed of
baskets of fruit and flowers
(photograph: the author)

6 – Roland Fréart de Chambray (1606-1676),
Callimachus' discovery of the Corinthian Order
(from Roland Fréart, Parallele de l'Architecture
Antique et de la Moderne *(Paris, 1650) 63)*

a return to the architectural simplicity of natural form, were of central importance to Shaftesbury and the 'new Junta'. In particular, Fréart's apology for truly ancient 'Greek' architecture was uniquely significant to this group.[73] In Ireland, this thinking was clearly known and promoted, with George Berkeley having declared that 'the old Romans were inferior to the Greeks, and ... the moderns fall infinitely short of both in the grandeur and *simplicity* of taste' after a visit to the Greek ruins of Sicily.[74] In these circumstances, it seems rather less than fanciful to suggest that this unique subversion of the Corinthian Order in Ireland to a state of complete natural simplicity was a means by which Castletown was philosophically situated at the very nexus of the promotion of Shaftesburian architectural thought in a way which would have been visually patent to a contemporary viewer of Molesworth's circle.

As with the seemingly anachronistic great hall, the presence of a long gallery (Plate 7) at first glance seems to be primarily a means of situating Conolly within the aristocratic ruling class. But, as with the iconographic messages in the hall, Conolly appears to have utilised the long gallery as a means of communicating more than this. During his tour of Ireland, John Loveday was keen to draw attention to the contents of the long gallery in addition to its grandeur.[75] It had been hung not with portraits of Conolly's ancestors, which would have been impossible given his lowly origins, but of his political allies: 'here is a Length of ye Duke of Wharton, another of ye Duke of Grafton Lord Lieutenant, and his Dutchess, but a remarkably good Length-Painting of Lord-Chancellor West, in his Robes', all centred on what was thought to be Garrett Morphey's portrait of King William III which, by family tradition, had been a gift to Conolly from the King himself.[76] This gallery of predominantly political portraits emphasised Conolly's associational links to notable heroes, military champions and great statesmen suggesting a strong allegiance to the Irish patriotic cause.[77] In this respect, the presence of a great hall and long gallery in what has been somewhat uncomfortably deemed a 'Palladian' house may arguably be a rational provision of the requisite tools of state for an Irish seigneurial landlord wishing to self-identify both with the ancient landowning class and with the very current conception of Irish 'improvement'.

The majority of writers have deemed Castletown to be 'Palladian' principally as a result of the colonnades and terminating pavilions flanking the main block of the house. Desmond Guinness has asserted that 'Classical colonnades were unknown in Ireland when Castletown was built'.[78] He argued that their dual purpose at Castletown – to house utilitarian yards linked in function to the estate farm rather than the house, and, by their

7 – The Long Gallery, Castletown, 1967
(*courtesy Irish Architectural Archive*)

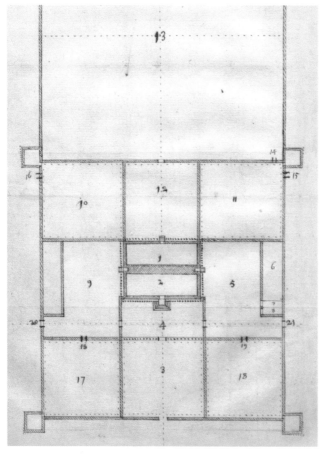

8 – 'A View of Part of the Honour of Burton in Ireland', 1737

This shows Burton House (in ruins following its destruction in the Williamite Wars) and its surrounding walled courtyards and gardens. (© British Library Board, Add. MS 47009 A f.27)

9 – Plan of Burton House and its surrounding walled courtyards and turrets, 1670

1. & 2. Burton House
3. The Forecourt 84 x 78 feet
4. "A gravl'd court" 84 x 36 feet "for taking coaches and their turning"
5. Stable court; 6. Stables
7. & 8. Two coach houses
9. A court containing a building 60 x 74 feet for brew house, bake house and wash house
10. A court 84 x 78 feet "to lay fyering in"
12. The back court entering the garden 80 x 76 feet
13. The pleasure gardens
17. & 18. Two "waste courts" 78 feet square
(© British Library Board, Add. MS 46948 f. 16b)

attachment to the house, increasing the impact and grandeur of its façade – became a novel, defining and unique feature of the Irish country house type based on Edward Lovett Pearce's study of Palladio in Italy.[79] Whilst it is clear that Pearce investigated this Palladian villa plan during his time in Italy, what is much more interesting is the question of whether this practical, economical and rational plan had, in fact, been developing naturally in Ireland independently of the influence of Palladio.[80] It is arguable that what Guinness has described as the 'economical Palladian plan' of Castletown, in fact, had begun to develop out of adapted defensive bawns as early as the seventeenth century. Originally composed of a simple walled enclosure with defensive towers at each corner, over time the bawn became less a purely defensive feature and more an economical and rational way of relating service buildings to the main house and enclosing formal and working gardens, which can be directly related to the later economic, compact country house plan.[81] Firstly, outbuildings were constructed along the defensive walls parallel to the gable ends of the main house, as at Perceval's Burton Park, near Mallow in county Cork, where two service buildings – one containing stables and the other a brew house, bake house and wash house – were constructed parallel to the main house within adjoining courtyards (Plates 8, 9). Whilst the unfortified house is surrounded by enclosed courtyards and bounded by a defensive wall with four battlemented turrets, the changing way in which these seemingly purely defensive complexes were being considered is clearly evidenced in correspondence from Perceval's builder, Thomas Smith, during construction.[82] The idea of constructing a fortified gate house is rejected on the basis that it would 'blinde the house', whilst the recommendation that the inner courtyard walls be built at a lower height than the outer curtain wall so that the house could be protected from any

10 – Entrance front at Springhill, county Derry, 1680-98
The projecting single-storey extensions with canted bays were added to the main seven-bay house c.1765, replacing
right-angled screen walls connecting the service pavilions to the house and forming a three-sided courtyard bawn.
(© National Trust Images / Matthew Antrobus)

11 – Elevations of the entrance and garden front at Shannongrove, county Limerick, 1709-20
L-shaped service pavilions extend the horizontal emphasis of the main house.
(courtesy Irish Architectural Archive)

opposite 12 – Willem van der Hagen (d.1745), VIEW OF CARTON HOUSE AS IT APPEARED IN *1687*
c.1690, oil on canvas (private collection)

two of the four turrets, 'should any Court be by enemy surpriz'd', may well have been trumped by the requirement that higher walls were 'better for wall fruit'.[83]

Eventually, elongated service buildings joined to the main body of the house by straight or curved screen walls replaced these parallel outer walls entirely. Any pretence at fortified protection was abandoned with the removal of the fourth enclosing wall, creating an open courtyard which could be enclosed with a wooden gate during times of unrest. This plan can be seen to have developed by the time Springhill in county Derry was constructed, with its open courtyard bounded on two sides by elegant curvilinear gabled service pavilions around 1697 (Plate 10). It is still in evidence at Shannongrove, county Limerick, completed around 1720, where the service pavilions are now constructed on an L-shaped plan, the longer arm running on the same axis as the main house, thus greatly increasing the horizontal impact of the entrance façade (Plate 11). Finola O'Kane has argued that Robert Molesworth himself retained elements of an earlier bawn at Breckdenston (near Swords, county Dublin) as late as 1716, and has also explored how Breckdenston's landscape design represented the interests of the 'New Junta'.[84]

The utility of the bawn in these late-seventeenth and early eighteenth-century houses was arguably threefold. Firstly, it demonstrated a physical connection between the landowner and his household and the working estate in a way which fitted the philosophical underpinnings of Irish 'improvement' and the archetype of the resident benevolent landlord at the heart of the estate. Secondly, situating eighteenth-century buildings within an ongoing project of 'improvement' which had started a century earlier communicated messages about the permanency and ongoing legitimacy of the Protestant ruling élite. Finally, and very much related to this, an antiquarian interest in past building types had both a personal and practical purpose in Irish country house building. Like Conolly's great hall and long gallery at Castletown, such references may have silenced any detractor tempted to impugn the settlers as upstarts. On a practical level, it was also much more economical to retain existing structures rather than building anew, particularly when those buildings could have formed an extra defensive measure if required, providing reassurance and peace of mind for the inhabitants.[85] Evidence of the potency of antiquarian interest in existing building types can be found with the improvements carried out by Sir Donat O'Brien at Leamaneh Castle, county Clare, in the years prior to his death in 1717 and the repair and refurnishing of Lohort Castle, county Cork, by the improving Perceval earls of Egmont between 1737 and 1752.[86] In this respect, seemingly anachronistic use of the 'bawn plan' may arguably have had significant personal and political currency in Ireland.

This developing 'bawn plan' could well have informed the plan of the original

Carton House, built close to the site of Castletown by James II's Catholic Lord Lieutenant in 1687, where it arguably reached its apotheosis (Plate 12). Here the service pavilions are presented on the main façade along a horizontal axis, joined to the main body of the house with curved screen walls, thus much increasing the width, impact and grandeur of the entrance front. Any pretence of a defensive purpose is all but abandoned in the decorative ironwork which encloses the vast courtyard.[87] Little scholarly investigation has been expended on the first Carton House of 1687, precisely because it seemed, on the one hand, to encompass a series of architectural features which were 'artisan mannerist' in style, yet nevertheless adopted what at Castletown was deemed to be a radical new 'Palladian' plan on the other. It was therefore very difficult to accommodate in any one architectural narrative, and challenged the primacy of Castletown as Ireland's first house built to this economic, compact plan. In appearance, however, the entrance front of Castletown owes infinitely more to the first Carton than any of Palladio's villas in its massing and the relationship between the main house and pavilions.

It is perhaps not at all fanciful to speculate that the opening of the enclosed bawns at Springhill, Shannongrove and especially Tyrconnell's Carton, each of which promoted an earlier concept of Irish 'improvement', are just as likely a source for the plan of Castletown in an ongoing but changing project of improvement as anything Pearce may have seen in Italy. In this paradigm, there is no conflict between the appearance and the seemingly anachronistic plan of the house, neither of which were designed to be read as novel or 'Palladian', but rather as economical, rational and most of all a uniquely Irish means of demonstrating how a good land steward in the unique cultural and economic circumstances of Ireland should arrange his house and, in doing so, promote Irish prosperity through financial and political independence.

Since academic interest in Castletown was first ignited by Desmond Guinness and Desmond FitzGerald in the 1960s, commentators have struggled to come to terms with its place, and indeed that of much Irish architecture of this period, in the narrative of architectural history. In concentrating upon authorship and style, these academics have arguably missed what was of most importance to those who conceived and constructed Castletown. When the eighteenth-century viewer critically assessed the value, meaning and 'Irishness' of Castletown, they did so not through a check-list of architectural features which stylistically related the building to similar projects in England or elsewhere. Instead, they sought an architecture, whatever its form might be, which would display and promote the philosophical and political conceptualisation of an ongoing, protean and uniquely Irish project of 'improvement'. Castletown's undeniable and pivotal importance in the corpus of Irish architecture, therefore, is not only to be found in the novelty of its appearance or 'style', but also in the role it had in displaying and promoting the axiomatic philosophical and political changes in Protestant self-fashioning and the conceptualisation of Irish 'improvement' which occurred in the first half of the eighteenth century. The building of a wholly new great house was the primary accomplishment, and its aesthetic then responded to a variety of motives – practical, aspirational and ideological. When taken in this context, seemingly anachronistic references and stylistic solecisms in its plan and appearance become instead a more calculated continuity, and differences between Irish and English architecture in the first half of the eighteenth-century are substantially explained in a way which does not cast Ireland as a provincial and *retardataire* artistic province in the shadow of England. Ireland is instead cast as a kingdom in which a uniquely Irish architecture, founded upon the protean principal of 'improvement', was flourishing and helped fashion the kingdom as distinct and independent among the states of Europe.

––––––

ENDNOTES

The following abbreviations are used: BL British Library
TCD Trinity College Dublin

[1]   See Desmond Guinness, '"We Have to Save it" – Castletown and the Irish Georgian Society', in Elizabeth Mayes (ed.), *Castletown, Decorative Arts* (OPW, Trim, 2011) 46-49; Desmond Guinness, *Castletown, Celbridge, Co. Kildare: formerly the home of the Conolly family now the headquarters of the Irish Georgian Society* (Celbridge, 1971); Sarah Conolly-Carew, *The Children of Castletown House* (Dublin, 2015) 192-202; Maurice Craig, *Castletown, Co. Kildare* (Celbridge, 1969); Patrick Walsh, *Castletown, Co. Kildare* (Dublin, 2007); Patrick Walsh, *The Making of the Irish Protestant Ascendancy: the life of William Conolly 1662-1729* (Woodbridge, 2010); Patrick Walsh and A.P.W. Malcomson, *The Conolly Archive* (Dublin, 2010).

[2]   Walsh, *The Making of the Irish Protestant Ascendancy*, 181.

[3]   Desmond FitzGerald, 'New Light on Castletown, Co. Kildare', *Quarterly Bulletin of the Irish Georgian Society*, VII, 1, 1965, 3-9; Maurice Craig and Desmond FitzGerald, 'Castletown, Co. Kildare', *Country Life*, CXLV, no. 3760, 27th March 1969, 722-26, no. 3761, 3rd April 1969, 798-802, and no. 3762, 10th April 1969, 882-85; Edward McParland, 'Eclecticism: The Provincial's Advantage', *Irish Arts Review Yearbook*, 1991, 210-13; Giles Worsley, 'Castletown, Co. Kildare', *Country Life*, CLXXXVIII, 11, 17th March 1994, 52-57.

[4]   See, for instance, Desmond Guinness and Charles Lines, *Castletown* [pamphlet] (Castletown, n.d.); Maurice Craig and John Cornforth, 'Castletown, Co. Kildare', *Irish Georgian Society Yearbook*, 1969; McParland, 'Eclecticism: The Provincial's Advantage', 210-13; Alistair Rowan, 'The Irishness of Irish Architecture', *Architectural History*, 40, 1997, 1-23; Timothy Mowl and Brian Earnshaw, *An Insular Rococo: Architecture, Politics and Society in Ireland and England 1710-1770* (London, 1999), especially at 13; Toby Barnard, *Making the Grand Figure: lives and possessions in Ireland 1641-1770* (Yale, 2004) 25-29; Eve Walsh Stoddard, *Positioning Gender and Race in (Post)colonial Plantation Space: Connecting Ireland and the Caribbean* (New York, 2012) 25-50.

[5]   McParland, 'Eclecticism: The Provincial's Advantage', 210.

[6]   BL, Add MS 47029, f.126, letter of George Berkeley to Lord Perceval, Dublin, 29th July 1722; BL, Add MS 4029, ff.129-30, letter of Lord Perceval to George Berkeley, Tunbridge, 5th August 1722.

[7]   BL, Add MS 4029, ff.129-30, letter of Lord Perceval to George Berkeley, Tunbridge, 5th August, 1722.

[8]   TCD, MS 2535, ff.65-66, letter of William King to Edward Southwell, Dublin, 21st January 1718.

[9]   Edward McParland, *Public Architecture in Ireland 1680-1760* (Yale, 2001); McParland, 'Eclecticism:

The Provincial's Advantage', 210-13; Worsley, 'Castletown, Co. Kildare', 52-57; Rowan, 'The Irishness of Irish Architecture', 13-14; Mowl and Earnshaw, *An Insular Rococo*, 126-146.

[10] See, for instance, Barbara Arciszewska, 'A Villa Fit for a King: The Role of Palladian Architecture in the Ascendancy of the House of Hanover under George I', *Revue d'Art Canadienne*, 19, nos 1-2, 1992, 41-58; Barbara Arciszewska, *The Hanoverian Court and the Triumph of Palladio: the Palladian revival in Hanover and England c.1700* (Warsaw, 2002); Barbara Arciszewska and Elizabeth McKellar (eds), *Articulating British Classicism: new approaches to eighteenth-century architecture* (London, 2004); Barbara Arciszewska, *Classicism and Modernity: architectural thought in eighteenth-century Britain* (Warsaw, 2010); Peter Burke, *Hybrid Renaissance: culture, language, architecture* (Budapest, 2016); Carole Fry, 'The Dissemination of Neo-Palladian Architecture in England', doctoral thesis, University of Bristol, 2006.

[11] Peter Burke, Hybrid Renaissance, 53-76.

[12] Alistair Rowan, 'The Irishness of Irish Architecture', 14-16.

[13] See, for instance, Jacqueline Genet (ed.), *The Big House in Ireland: reality and representation* (Dingle, 1991); Malcolm Kelsall, *Literary Representations of the Irish Country House* (London 2003); Daniel Maudlin, 'Early Colonial Architecture', in G.A. Bremner (ed.), *Architecture and Urbanism in the British Empire* (Oxford, 2016) 19-50: 43-45; Arthur Parkinson, Mark Scott and Declan Redmond, 'Negotiating Postcolonial Legacies: shifting conservation narratives and residual colonial build heritage in Ireland', *Town Planning Review*, 86, no. 2, 2015, 203-28; Terence Dooley, 'The Destruction of the Country House in Ireland, 1879-1973', in James Raven (ed.), *Lost Mansions: essays on the destruction of the country house* (London, 2015) 44-62; Stoddard, *Positioning Gender and Race in (Post)colonial Plantation Space,* 25-50.

[14] Ciaran Brady and Jane Ohlmeyer, 'Making Good: new perspectives on the English in modern Ireland', in *idem* (eds), *British Interventions in Early Modern Ireland* (Cambridge, 2004) 1-27; Toby Barnard, 'Interests in Ireland: the "Fanatic Zeal and Irregular Ambition" of Richard Lawrence', in Brady and Ohlmeyer, *British Interventions in Early Modern Ireland*, 299-314; Toby Barnard, *Improving Ireland? Projectors, Prophets and Profiteers, 1641-1786* (Dublin, 2008); Alan Houston, *Benjamin Franklin and the Politics of Improvement* (Yale, 2008); Kevin Sharpe, *Remapping Early Modern England: the culture of seventeenth-century politics* (Cambridge, 2000); Paul Slack, *The Invention of Improvement: information and material progress in seventeenth-century England* (Oxford, 2014).

[15] Houston, *Benjamin Franklin and the Politics of Improvement*, 12-13.

[16] Barnard, *Improving Ireland?*, 12-14

[17] Slack, *The Invention of Improvement*, 1.

[18] *ibid.*, 8-9.

[19] Richard Lawrence, *The interest of Ireland in its trade and wealth stated* (Dublin, 1682); Robert Molesworth, *The True Way to Render Ireland Happy & Secure: OR A Discourse wherein it is shewn that 'tis the interest of England and Ireland to Encourage Foreign Protestants to Plant in Ireland* (Dublin, 1697).

[20] Samuel Madden, *Reflections and Resolutions Proper for the Gentlemen of Ireland as to their Conduct for the Service of their Country* (Dublin, 1738), see in particular vii; A.P.W. Malcomson, 'Absenteeism in Eighteenth-Century Ireland', *Irish Economic and Social History*, I, no. 1, 1974, 15-35.

[21] *ibid.*, 3.

[22] *ibid.*

[23] *ibid.*, 10.

24 Barnard, 'Interests in Ireland', 302.

25 Anon., *The Present State of Ireland together with some Remarques upon the Ancient State thereof. Likewise a Description of the Chief Towns. With a Map of the Kingdome* (London, 1673) 214.

26 *ibid.*, 276.

27 John Dunton, *Teague Land or A Merry Ramble to the Wild Irish 1698* (Dublin, 2003) 122.

28 Anon., *The Present State of Ireland*, 205-06.

29 Barnard, 'Interests in Ireland', 299.

30 *ibid.*, 299-306.

31 Richard Lawrence, *The Interest of England in the Irish Transplantation* (London, 1655); Richard Lawrence, *England's Great Interest in the Well Planting of Ireland* (Dublin, 1656).

32 Richard Lawrence, *The Interest of Ireland in its Trade and Wealth Stated* (Dublin, 1682) 37-39.

33 Barnard, 'Interests in Ireland', 304.

34 Francis G. James, 'Irish Colonial Trade in the Eighteenth Century', *The William and Mary Quarterly*, 20, no. 4, October 1963, 574-84; Patrick Kelly, 'The Irish Woollen Export Prohibition Act of 1699: Kearney Revisited', *Irish Economic and Social History*, 7, no. 1, 1980, 22-44: 24-26.

35 William Molyneux, *The Case of Ireland being Bound by Act of Parliament in England Stated by William Mollyneux of Dublin Esq.* (London, 1770) 10-13.

36 *ibid.*

37 *ibid.*, 14.

38 *ibid.*

39 *ibid.*, 29.

40 Robert, Viscount Molesworth, *An Account of Denmark as it was in the Year 1692* (London, 1692) preface.

41 BL, Add MS 47027, f.16, letter of George Berkeley to Sir John Perceval, London, 26th January 1713.

42 Christ Church College Oxford, Wake Papers, XIV, no. 214, letter of William King, 8th June 1723.

43 TCD, MS 2533/273, letter of William King to Robert Molesworth, August 1716. See also Joseph Richardson, 'Archbishop William King (1650-1729): Church Tory and State Whig?', *Eighteenth-Century Ireland / Iris an dá Chultúr*, 15, 2000, 54-76.

44 National Library of Ireland, Microfilm p.3753, letter of Robert, Viscount Molesworth to John Molesworth, London, 20th October 1722.

45 TCD, MS 2533, f.110, letter of William King to Mr Standhope, Dublin, 1st November, 1715.

46 Walsh, *The Making of the Irish Protestant Ascendancy*, 169-70.

47 See BL, Add MS 47027, ff.16-282, the correspondence of George Berkeley and Sir John Perceval; McParland, 'Eclecticism: The Provincial's Advantage', 211.

48 See John Gerald Simms, *Colonial Nationalism 1698-1776: Molyneux's The State of Ireland – Stated* (Dublin, 1976) 24-36.

49 BL, Add MS 47029, f.126, letter of George Berkeley to John, Viscount Perceval, Dublin, 29th July 1722.

50 See Irish Architectural Archive, 2008/44/92, Edward McParland, 'Edward Lovett Pearce and the New Junta for Architecture in Eighteenth-Century Ireland', lecture given at the University of Notre Dame, Indiana, October 1991; Edward McParland, 'Sir Thomas Hewett and the New Junta for Architecture', in Giles Worsley (ed.), *The Role of the Amateur Architect* (London, 1994) 21-26; Edward McParland, 'Edward Lovett Pearce and the New Junta for Architecture', in Toby Barnard and Jane Clark (eds), *Lord Burlington, Architecture, Art and Life* (London, 1995) 151-66.

51 Anthony, Earl of Shaftesbury, 'A Letter Concerning the Art or Science of Design Written from Italy on the Occasion of the Judgment of Hercules to My Lord Somers, Naples, March 6 1712', in Anthony,

Earl of Shaftesbury, *Characteristicks of Men, Manners, Opinions, Times*, 3 vols (London, 1732, Bodleian Library copy) III, 95-410. Though penned in 1712, it has been suggested that the letter was not published before 1732 after Conolly's death. However, given that many of those who surrounded Conolly had close personal connections to Shaftesbury, it seems highly likely that he was aware of its content when he commenced plans for Castletown in 1719. See Kerry Downes, 'The Publication of Shaftesbury's "Letter Concerning Design" ', *Architectural History*, 27, 1984, 519-23; Alexander Echlin and William Kelley, 'A "Shaftesburian Agenda"? Lord Burlington, Lord Shaftesbury and the intellectual origins of English Palladianism', *Architectural History*, 59, January 2016, 221-52: 225.

[52] Letter from Anthony, Earl of Shaftesbury to Robert Molesworth, Beachworth, 12th January 1708, in John Toland (ed.), *Letters from the Right Honourable the Late Earl of Shaftesbury to Robert Molesworth Esq. Now the Lord Viscount of that Name* (London, 1721) 25-28: 26.

[53] Shaftesbury, 'A Letter Concerning the Art or Science of Design', 398.

[54] *ibid.*, 400.

[55] *ibid.*, 401-02.

[56] John Summerson, *Architecture in Britain 1530-1830* (Yale, 1993) 293-309. Catherine Arbuthnott, 'Kent's Patrons', in S. Weber (ed.), *William Kent: Designing Georgian Britain* (Yale, 2013) 63-70.

[57] Summerson, *Architecture in Britain*, 293-309. See also John Wilton-Ely, *Apollo of the Arts: Lord Burlington and his circle* (Nottingham, 1973) 7; Dana Arnold, 'It's a Wonderful Life', in *idem* (ed.), *Belov'd by Evr'y Muse: Richard Boyle 3rd Earl of Burlington and 4th Earl of Cork (1694-1753)*, (London, 1994) 5-14: 5; Timothy Mowl, *William Kent: Architect, Designer, Opportunist* (London, 2006).

[58] Vaughan Hart, *Nicholas Hawksmoor: Rebuilding Ancient Wonders* (London, 2007) 33. See Dana Arnold, *Architectural Aesthetics: interpreting Classical antiquity in the eighteenth century* (London, 2013).

[59] Shaftesbury, 'A Letter Concerning the Art or Science of Design, 402.

[60] Rowan, 'The "Irishness" of Irish Architecture', 14-15.

[61] Shaftesbury, 'A Letter Concerning the Art or Science of Design, 404-05.

[62] Echlin and Kelley, 'A Shaftesburian Agenda', 221-52.

[63] *ibid.*, 233.

[64] Letter of Anthony, Earl of Shaftesbury to Robert Molesworth, Beachworth, 12th January 1708, in John Toland (ed.), *Letters from the Right Honourable the Late Earl of Shaftesbury to Robert Molesworth Esq. Now the Lord Viscount of that Name* (London, W. Wilkins, 1721) 25-28: 26, wherein Shaftesbury exclaims that Molesworth had 'long had [his] Heart, even before [he] knew [him] personally' as a result of his admiration of The State of Denmark.

[65] See McParland, 'Edward Lovett Pearce and the New Junta for Architecture in Eighteenth-Century Ireland'; McParland, 'Sir Thomas Hewett and the New Junta for Architecture'; McParland, 'Edward Lovett Pearce and the New Junta for Architecture', 151-166. This argument is also made by Echlin and Kelley, 'A Shaftesburian Agenda', 228-33.

[66] McParland, 'Eclecticism: The Provincial's Advantage', 210.

[67] Shaftesbury, 'A Letter Concerning the Art or Science of Design, 400.

[68] See, for instance, Charles Topham Bowden, *A Tour through Ireland* (Dublin, 1791) 68, where Castletown is described as 'the Seat, or rather Palace, of the Rt. Hon. Mr Conolly', and, more patently, the letter of Alessandro Galilei to Robert, Viscount Molesworth of 1719 wherein he states that he is working on '*i desegni d'un Palazzo di Villa p.il My Lord Governatore di quell regno*'. See Ilaria Toesca, 'Alessandro Galilei in Inghilterra', in Mario Praz (ed.), *English Miscellany*, 30 vols (Rome, 1952) III, 213.

[69] See, in particular, McParland, 'Eclecticism: The Provincial's Advantage', 210-213; Rowan, 'The 'Irishness' of Irish Architecture', 14-16; Stoddard, *Positioning Gender and Race in (Post)colonial Plantation Space*, 25-50.

[70] David Cast, 'Seeing Vanbrugh and Hawksmoor', *Journal of the Society of Architectural Historians*, vol. 43, no. 4, December 1984, 310-27: 321-22; Andor Gomme and Alison Maguire, *Design and Plan in the Country House: from castle donjons to Palladian boxes* (Yale, 2008) 148.

[71] Philip Luckombe, *A Tour through Ireland* (London, 1783) 42. For contemporary criticisms of Conolly's lowly origins, see Letter from Sir John St. Leger, Baron of the Exchequer in Ireland, to Lord Chief Justice Parker, Dublin, 21st February 1717, BL, Add MS 750 and 244 (Stowe Papers); Jonathan Swift, 'A Short Character of His Excellency Thomas Earl of Wharton, Lord Lieutenant of Ireland, with an Account of some smaller facts during his Government which will not be put into the Articles of Impeachment', in Jonathan Swift, *The Works of Jonathan Swift D.D., Dean of St Patrick's, Dublin*, IV (Edinburgh, 1824) 3-29: 28; Letter of Jonathan Swift to John Gay and the Duchess of Queensbury, Powerscourt, 28 August 1731, in F. Elrington Ball (ed.), *The Correspondence of Jonathan Swift, D.D.*, IV (London, 1913) 258; John Trenchard, 'A Letter from a Soldier to the Commons of England Occasioned by an Address now carrying on by the Protestants in Ireland in order to take away the Fund Appropriated for the Payment of the Army', in *A Collection of State Tracts Publish'd during the Reign of King William III*, II (London, 1706) 773-87: 785-86.

[72] Roland Fréart, *Parallel of the Antient Architecture with the Modern* (trans. John Evelyn), (London, 1664) 62-65.

[73] See Echlin and Kelley, 'A Shaftesburian Agenda', 229-33.

[74] Letter of George Berkeley to Lord Perceval, Rome, 28th July 1718, transcribed in Benjamin Rand (ed.), *Berkeley and Percival: The Correspondence of George Berkeley afterwards Bishop of Cloyne and Sir John Percival afterwards Earl of Egmont* (Cambridge, 1914) 171-73: 172. See Echlin and Kelley, 'A Shaftesburian Agenda', 228-32.

[75] John Loveday, *Diary of a Tour in 1732 through parts of England, Wales, Ireland and Scotland* (London, 1890) 49-50.

[76] *ibid.*, 50.

[77] Kate Retford, *The Art of Domestic Life: family portraiture in 18th-century England* (Yale, 2006) 166.

[78] Guinness and Lines, *Castletown*, 4.

[79] *ibid.*

[80] RIBA Library, cat. no. 2385#, Andrea Palladio, *I Quatro Libri dell'Architettura di Andrea Palladio* (Venice, 1601) annotated by Edward Lovett Pearce during his tour of Italy 1723-24.

[81] Maurice Craig, *Classic Irish Houses of the Middle Size* (Dublin, 2006) 62.

[82] BL, Add MS 46948, ff.16b-17.

[83] *ibid.*, f.17.

[84] Finola O'Kane, *Landscape Design in Eighteenth-Century Ireland: mixing foreign trees with the natives* (Cork, 2004) 10-45.

[85] Barnard, *Improving Ireland*, 123-26.

[86] Finola O'Kane, 'Leamaneh and Dromoland: the O'Brien ambition, Part I: "Improvements ... not so Inconsiderable": the O'Briens' Baroque landscape at Leamaneh Castle, county Clare', *Irish Architectural and Decorative Studies*, VII, 2004, 64-79; Barnard, *Improving Ireland*, 125-42.

[87] Patricia McCarthy, *Life in the Country House in Georgian Ireland* (London, 2016) 12-14.

———

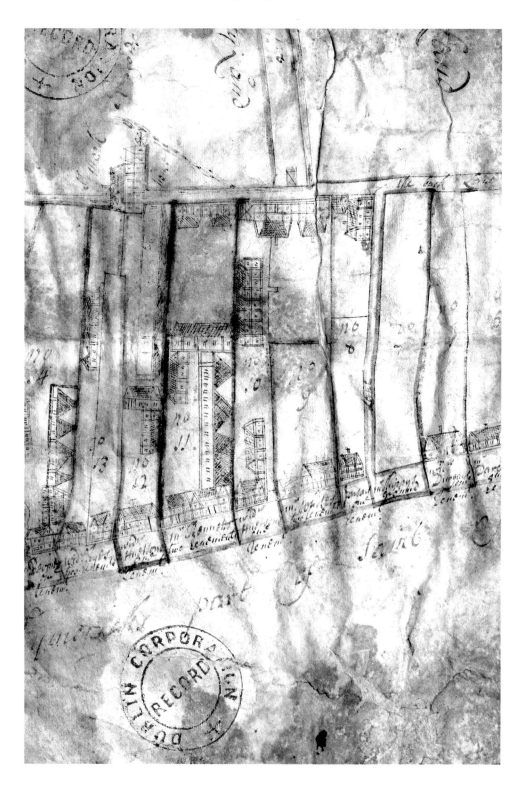

A Dublin streetscape in 1703:
an urban legacy of the Dongan estate

NEIL CRIMMINS

WILLIAM CONOLLY BOUGHT THE CASTLETOWN ESTATE AFTER HE HAD MADE HIS fortune elsewhere. He purchased it from Thomas Dongan in 1709 to have a base for entertaining near Dublin, one that would impress visitors who made the easy journey westwards along the river Liffey. Since 1588 Castletown had been controlled by the Dongan family, who held land in Kildare, with its great country manors and demesnes, as well as in Dublin's south-western quarter. There, at the west end of James's Street, they owned a block of modest townhouses with associated water-reliant industrial enterprises such as tanneries and breweries. Their dealings with the city council, particularly in respect of the watercourse that ran behind their block of land, led to founding of a workhouse at the block's western end. This eventually became St James's hospital. While the Conolly family benefited from Ireland's complex seventeenth-century history with its great shifts in religious and regal allegiances and their associated impact on Ireland's property mosaic, the Dongans did not. By 1709 the financial security and social position that had enabled the Dongan family to buy and live at Castletown since 1588 had dissipated. The Dongans' spatial legacy lies primarily in their Dublin city block, which still retains much of its seventeenth-century grain and some of its early eighteenth-century houses and their panelled interiors.

There are records of de Donjons or Dongans or Dungans in Ireland since the thirteenth century.[1] A John Dongan (c.1546-1592) was the son of a fishmonger, Edward (Thady) Dongan, from whom John inherited several properties in Dublin, including the family house on Fishamble Street. As a young man John Dongan acted as attorney for Thomas Butler, the Earl of Ormonde, becoming 'the hub of the wheel on which the treasury of Ireland revolved',[2] and also serving on Dublin Corporation as an alderman. These positions, though not well paid, enabled social and financial advancement, and John

---

1 – Detail of map dated 11th June 1703 accompanying 'Agreement between Earl of Limerick and Dublin Corporation dated 20 April 1705' showing the strip elevation of the Dongan block (see Plate 4) (courtesy Dublin City Library & Archive, Ancient Revenue 27)

Dongan accumulated substantial property both within the city and further afield. Dongan's property dealings were helped by the fact that exchequer officials were exempt from taxation. He, along with Thomas Cotton of England, was granted a twenty-one-year lease of numerous lands within The Pale, including possession of the Abbey of St Thomas the Martyr, Dublin, in 1577. In 1588 Thomas FitzGerald of Lackagh, county Kildare, and Edward FitzGerald, his brother, conveyed the lands and castles of Kildrought, Castletown and Kilmacredock in Kildare, to Thomas Alen, John Davies and Edward Dongan for the use and interest of John Dongan during his life, with the remainder to John's sons Walter, William and Edward and their heirs.[3] In a deed dated 20th December 1598, William Dongan swapped 'houses and other premises in the city of Dublin' for 'lands and tenements in Kildrought and Castletown of Kildrought', although it is not clear whether this included the manor of Castletown. John Dongan died, possibly of plague, in 1592, and in his will left '4 messuages and a domicile and garden called "The Grange" in St. James parish of Dublin' to his eldest son Walter.[4]

Sir Walter Dongan was the first of his family to live at the castle of Castletown. He bought a baronetcy for over £1,000 in 1622 and became Sherriff of Dublin in 1624, dying two years later in 1626.[5] Walter's heir was his eldest son Sir John Dongan, who married Mary, daughter of Sir William Talbot, first Baronet of Carton. The family had supported King Charles I, and as a consequence lost their estates under Cromwell. Sir John's first son, Walter, was a militant Catholic and one of the Irish chieftains who formed the Confederacy of Catholics at Kilkenny in 1646 and who fled to France after the Cromwellian war. On the restoration of Charles II in 1660, he was 'one of the few of the old Irish gentry to be restored to his estates'.[6] William succeeded his brother Walter in the baronetcy, and was created Viscount Dongan of Clane in 1662 and 1st Earl of Limerick in 1686.[7] He fought on the side of James II at the Battle of the Boyne, and following defeat he too retired to France. Outlawed for high treason, his estates were forfeited to King William III, who granted them to his favourite, the successful general de Ginkel, Earl of Athlone on 13th October, 1693.[8] The forfeited estates amounted to '26,480 acres, including the lands of Castletown, the manor of Kildraught, many other lands in the counties of Kildare, Dublin, Carlow, Meath, Kilkenny, Longford, Tipperary and Queen's County [now Laois]' and, significantly for this paper, 'several houses in Dublin and many tithes'.[9] When William Dongan – who had lost his only son, Walter, in the Battle of the Boyne – died in 1698, his younger brother Thomas (1634-1715) inherited the family estates and titles.

Thomas Dongan, 2nd Earl of Limerick was a well-travelled man. In 1667 Charles II gave him a pension of £500 per annum and a position in the army in consideration of his loyalty and associated losses. When Charles II ordered all English soldiers to leave the French Service in 1677, Dongan obediently left his lucrative colonelcy in the Irish Regiment.[10] After a brief and successful spell as deputy governor of Tangier, a 'dower' of his Portuguese wife, he was made governor of New York by James II on 30th September 1682.[11] The first Irish and only Catholic colonial governor of New York, Dongan established manors, 'about half of all those ever granted in New York',[12] and granted a number of large land patents for which he received substantial fees and bribes. Distinguishing himself as 'one of the province's greediest officials,' he notably gave Albany a charter that enlarged the city's limits by six miles northwards and included pastures south of the town over which the city's claims 'for a valuable consideration' were questionable.[13] Governor Dongan also made peace with the Five Nations of warlike Indians, and in 1687 took them under his protection in a war with French Canada. By his own account, Dongan was so successful in this role that had he not been dismissed from his post in 1688, he would have sent the Canadians

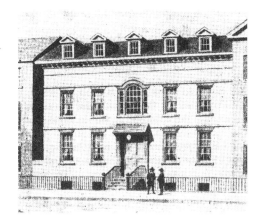

2 – New York house of Thomas Dongan, 2nd Earl of Limerick
from THE MEMORIAL HISTORY OF THE CITY OF NEW YORK, VOLUME 1 (New York History Company, 1892) 403

back to France. Eventually usurped by the Dutch Protestant interest in New York, Dongan had his American houses and other property seized, his servants imprisoned, and his estates confiscated (Plate 2).[14]

Returning to Ireland after his many sojourns abroad, Thomas Dongan claimed that he was legally entitled to his brother's estate but could not recover it because the settlement papers had been lost in the war.[15] However, in December 1700 Dongan found the papers and petitioned Parliament for relief in 1701, which they duly granted in 1702 but with punitive conditions: Dongan should not be entitled to any arrears of rent (worth over £6,000) nor should he be restored to the Rectories and Tithes part of the estate (worth £700 per annum); he should pay any people who had purchased parts of the estate under the Earl of Athlone two-thirds of their purchase money (£8,400); and he should not let nor sell his estate to anyone but Protestants. (Dongan claimed that this was abused by the Protestant tenants who would not pay their previous rents and by Protestant purchasers who would not pay the prices they had formerly offered.)[16] He calculated that the losses incurred by these conditions amounted to over £20,000, and that, in addition, he had not been paid his pension since 1688 and had lost over £10,000 in the war against the French Canadians. He was unsuccessful in his petition for compensation. A letter to an unknown addressee, written in this period, illuminated his position:

> I have been offering to sell lands since I gott the estate, but the purchasors from my Lord Athlone hindered severall people from purchasing from me, and from giving me money ... Coll Long was so kind, notwithstanding all the endeavours used against me as to lend me ... money ... but I am forced to give my Lord Chief Baron [Robert Rochfort] a lease for Castletown for seven years at his own rate ... I believe you are not of the opinion that it's fitt for a man to be laying out all he can scrape

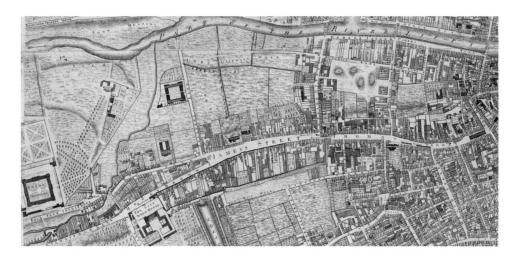

3 – John Rocque, AN EXACT SURVEY OF THE CITY
AND SUBURBS OF DUBLIN, 1757
detail of the south-western quarter of the city

opposite 4 – Map from 1703 accompanying the
'Agreement between Earl of Limerick and
Dublin Corporation', including strip elevation of the
Dongan block (DCLA, Ancient Revenue 27)

5 – Diagram of the plots shown in the 1703 map
of the Dongan block and the accompanying
legend of leaseholders

6 – John Rocque, DUBLIN, 1757
Detail of St James's Street showing the city workhouse as
built and with the 1703 plot holdings coloured. (This map
has been rotated to the same orientation as Plates 4 and 9.)

out the rotten estate in interest and continuall law suits if possibly he could get a purchasor. I have not gott 200 pounds out of the estate since I gott it and half of that Ms. Betty Cook had. As soon as I gott purchasors which I am labouring to find, she shall be the first creditor I'll pay, she being more troublesome to me than most...[17]

Dongan also looked to his Dublin city properties for some relief, in particular a block of land lying on the south side of James's Street and immediately north of the Earl of Meath's substantial estate that covered much of the city's south-western quarter (Plate 3). It lay west of the medieval city where James's Street and Thomas Street formed part of what was the *Slighe Mór*, an ancient route that led to the west of Ireland.[18] At St James's church the street widened to approximately twenty metres, much wider than usual and similar to its modern dimension. This suggests that it may have been a junction of three roads – James's Street, Bow Lane and Crocker's Lane. A medieval 'metalled' surface (formed from small 'sub-rounded' and angular pebbles beaten in place with sections of cobbles), which has recently been discovered here under a *c*.1700 cobbled road, may have been intended for a marketplace.[19] In the sixteenth century a successful fair was held annually over six days on this widened section of the street between the Dongan block and the church. Beginning on 25th June (St James's Day), it attracted merchants from England, France and Flanders.[20]

2015 copy by the author of
'*A Mapp of Severall parcells
of land, houses, outhouses,
orchards & gardens in Saint
James Streete... parish of the
same and suburb of the City
of Dublin belonging to the
Rt. Hon'able Thomas Earle
of Limerick and survey'd
by order of said Earle, the
eleventh day of June 1703
by me ....*'
[illegible signature, possibly Duffy]

City Land

Citty Land

A piece of land exchanged by the Rt. Hon'able the Earle of Limerick with the City whereon the hospital is building

1   Mr Shippy's 1 tenement
2   Mr Howard's 1 tenement
3   Mr Malone's 3 tenements
4   Mr Cusack's 2 tenements
5   Mr Darcey's 1 tenement
6   Mr Duignan's 1 tenement
7   Mr Shippy's ground

8   Mr Jonson's 1 tenement
9   Mr White's 2 tenements
10   Widow Hewetson's 1
      tenement
11   Mr Bennett's 2 tenements
12   Widow Huston's? 2
      tenements

13   Widow ....?
      2 tenements
14   ....? 1 tenement
15   Mr Howard's 2 tenements
16   Mr Brookfield's 1 tenement
17   Mr Bennett's 3 tenements
18   Mr Fenton's 1 tenement

Citty Land

19   Mr Jones's 3 tenements
20   Mr Shippy's 3 tenements
21   Widow Jonson's 1 tenement
22   Widow Stones's 8
      tenements

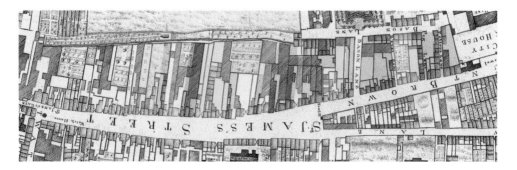

45

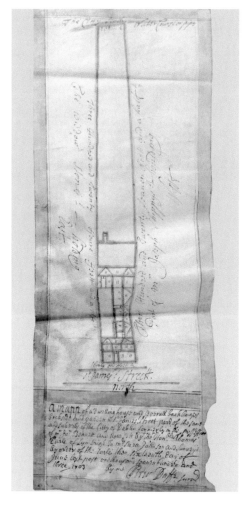

An extraordinary surviving map, dated 11th June 1703, reveals the urban block's architectural and spatial character (Plate 4). Containing also the only known drawing of an early eighteenth-century Dublin street elevation (Plate 1), the map described a well-built-up city block with a virtually unbroken street frontage extending from the site of the city workhouse, 'whereon the hospital is building', to a large piece of 'City ground' (later called the Pigeon Park). With the family embroiled in legal disputes when it was made, the map's primary intention was to record Thomas Dongan, 2nd Earl of Limerick's tenancies (Plate 5). The block's eastern end was bounded to the south by the city watercourse, and a water mill was located behind plots 11 and 12 (now nos 32-33 James's Street). The line of the watercourse corresponded to the boundary of the Earl of Meath's Liberty, with the water continuing west for a few plots before turning south. The line continued westward as 'the Back Lane', and many of the plots fronting onto James's Street also contained smaller buildings that fronted onto this lane. Archaeological investigations have dated the block's burgage plots and a field boundary to the mid-thirteenth century.[21] The map refers to the plots as

7 – 'A Map of a Dwelling House and Severall backhouses, backyard and garden in St. James's Street ... 1703 by me Peter Duffe Surveyor'.
This holding corresponds to plot 21 on the 1703 map (Plate 5), and is now part of Guinness Brewery. (courtesy National Archives of Ireland)

8 – St James's Street today

opposite 9 – Wide Street Commissioners 1799 plan of the block (courtesy DCLA, WSC 729) tenements, with many of them containing 'backsides, backhouses, gardens and yards'. Illegible in parts, the map listed the tenancies and 'quality' of each of twenty-two plots as well as its front and rear dimensions and length from front to rear.[22] The drawings of the buildings appear representative of actual structures, with the base of each building drawn at the line of the street (Plates 5, 6). By relating the map to the archways, lanes and streets that appear in later maps, and by comparing deeds of sale and lease (which sometimes list occupiers, their trades and give descriptions of the holdings) with the plots as described and drawn on the map, a picture of this section of James's Street in 1703 emerges. Contemporary lease maps of some of the properties confirm the general arrangement of the plots with outhouses to the rear, accessed from the street through archways in the gabled fronted houses and long gardens stretching back as far as the watercourse (Plate 7).

Disputes with the city over the Earl of Limerick's title to lands in Kildrought, county Kildare, had run concurrently with disputes over the St James's Street water rights since the 1660s. In 1703 a dispute arose between the Corporation and the earl, whose tenants freely drew water for their industries (mainly tanning and malting). The final ceding of the workhouse lands by Limerick formed part of a 1705 agreement whereby the Corporation gave up its counter claim to the Kildrought lands.[23] Although the lease is hard to read, an accompanying letter from the City Hall law agent Ignatius J. Rice to John J. Murphy Esq., Town Clerk, referred to original documents enclosed. One of them, dated 16th October 1703, between the Corporation and the Earl of Limerick,

> witnesses that the Corporation conveys to the Earl of Limerick in exchange certain lands in Killdrought and Killdrangan in the county of Kildare in fee simple, and the Earl of Limerick in exchange conveys to the Corporation in fee simple part of the lands enclosed by a stone wall at the upper end of St. James' St. on the South side of the road leading to Kilmainham, and the land with outside of the said wall

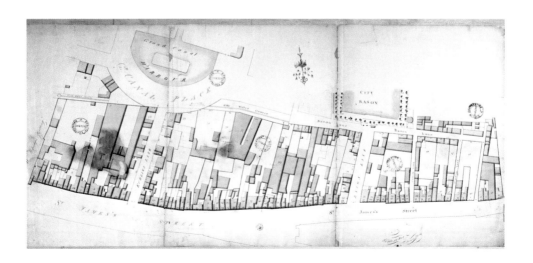

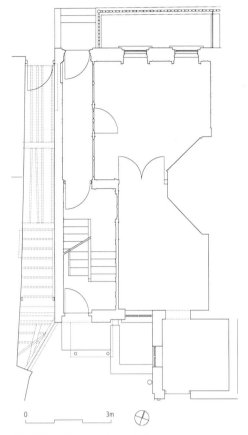

10 – Plan of No. 25 James's Street
with side passage (drawing: the author)

below 11 – Detail of panelling in No. 25 James's
Street (photo: the author)

opposite 12 – Detail of the panelling in the Brown
Study, Castletown House (photo: the author)

on the North end thereof extending from the said wall to pavement, and in breadth equal to the said lands of the said Earl enclosed within the said wall from East to West lying and being in the parish of St. James and City of Dublin, which ground is designed by the city for a public charity.[24]

The 1703 map also related to an agreement by the Earl to cede the watercourse to the Corporation in exchange for perpetual rights to water for his tenants.[25] The lease agreement between the Corporation and Thomas Dongan, Earl of Limerick stated:

whereas several disputes have arisen in relation to part of the city watercourse running from the south part of the Said Earle of Limericks tenements and gardens in St James's Street, Dublin and in relation to that part of the ground whereon the city ... lately built a stone wall for the preservation of the said watercourse ... have mutually agreed that the said Thomas Earle of Limerick should release or convey to the said city for ever all right or title which he pretends to have to that part of the ground whereon the said wall is now built with liberty to build up the same as high as they shall think fitt and to carry on the same in a straight line on the north banks of the said course as far as they shall think fitt without interruption of the said Earle or any claiming under him ... provided the foundation of any wall ... shall take up no more ... than the foundation of the present wall...[26]

The Corporation granted to Limerick and his tenants 'a proportionable share' of water to the 'present tenements forever', specified as that provided by a pipe of two inches to 'tan-yards, skinners yards or in dressing skinns or leather', a pipe of one and a half inch bore to 'public brewhouses or malthouses', and a pipe of three-quarters of an inch bore 'to every other house ... without paying any rent'.[27]

The origin of Dublin's modern St James's Hospital is the 'hospital' or workhouse that was built on 'a piece of land exchanged by the Right Hon'ble the Earle of Limerick with the City' (Plates 3, 6). William, Earl of Limerick had initially granted the land for the workhouse and was also on the committee to fund the workhouse with a corn toll.[28] The City Assembly rolls of 1669 had noted that the late King James and the Earl of Limerick had each given land near St James's Street, and that the city joined another parcel on the road to Kilmainham.[29] When William of Orange gave Limerick's estate to de Ginkel, Earl of Athlone, he was obliged to keep to the earlier agreement and allow the workhouse to be built on this ground. The Dublin Assembly Roll of 1697 described how Dublin city 'swarm[ed] with beggars, who, for want of learning to get their livelyhood,' had ' become a great nuisance' and would 'more and more increase if some course be not taken to put them to worke.' The planned workhouse was ' built to put idlers to worke in' observing that 'the late wars [had] prevented soe good a design.' It also described the 'place without St. James Gate, whereof belongs to the right honorable the earle of Athlone and part to this citty, which was intended for that purpose and well enclosed with a stone wall'. Nothing was wanting 'but a fund to build the same'.[30]

While the eighteenth century saw the successful establishment of St James's Hospital on the site west of the Dongan block, the gable fronts depicted on the 1703 map street elevation were soon replaced with more fashionable parapets. Generally the area's smaller breweries and distilleries were taken over by the larger ones, leading to the eventual total control of this water-dependant industry by the Guinness family, whose brewery now extends into the east end of this block. A Wide Streets Commissioners' map of c.1800 lists No. 28 James's Street as 'Arthur Guinness's dwelling house formerly a distillery and yards' (Plate 9 [plot 10 in 1703 map, Plates 4, 5]). There may be traces of timbers from the earlier cagework houses, and some possible earlier basements hidden within the existing buildings on the block. No. 25 James's Street contains evidence of early timbers in its side passage, a potentially early basement, and a roof which appears to be of a transitional type between the Dutch Billy and the later more common double A-roof with parapet (Plate 10). This house also has early eighteenth-century raised and fielded panelling, which is similar in profile, if not in grandeur, to that of the panelled room in Castletown that dates from the same period (Plates 11, 12).

On 21st September 1709, Thomas Dongan, Earl of Limerick conveyed Castletown to William Conolly for a 'consideration of £15,000'.[31] It was a complex legal transaction as many of Dongan's holdings in Kildare and Dublin continued to be encumbered by numerous debts, mortgages and leases. William Conolly stated that Dongan had

> granted, bargained, sold released and confirmed unto me the said William Conolly my Heires and Assignes for Ever All that and those the Mannors Lordships Castles Towns and Lands of Castletowne, Kildraught, Kilmacredock Coolmacthomas, Parts of Donaughmoor Collinstownes Collinblackstowne, Godfriharristowne Moortowne and Possetown all situate lying and being in the County of Kildare'.[32]

So began the Conolly period at Castletown. Thomas Dongan continued to part with parcels of his estate, selling some of his American properties, including an estate on Staten Island to three great-nephews who had settled there in 1711. He died in London on 14th December 1715 and is buried in St Pancras churchyard.[33]

The Dongan and Conolly influence over areas of Dublin's architectural heritage has not been substantially researched and the legal bargaining and swapping that accounted for the formation (and break-up) of Dublin's urban estates is not well understood. While Dongan's forced sale of Castletown resulted in the building of a great house and estate, the piecemeal selling off of his properties in James's Street resulted in much more modest developments. The fragmented nature of these plots and complicated ownership patterns, as well as the industrial nature of the area, inhibited the type of large-scale development that occurred elsewhere in Dublin later in the eighteenth century. As a result, this area has been substantially overlooked and undervalued as part of Dublin's Georgian history.

———

ENDNOTES

The following abbreviations are used:

CARD   *The Calendar of Ancient Records of Dublin* *

DCLA   Dublin City Library & Archive

*   Sir John Thomas Gilbert (1829-1898) was an Irish archivist, antiquarian and historian who, amongst other works, including *A History of the City of Dublin in three volumes*, transcribed (with his widow, who continued the later volumes) the Assembly Rolls of the City of Dublin 1447-1841. The Rolls record the minutes of the Dublin City Assembly. These transcriptions can be viewed in *The Calendar of Ancient Records of Dublin* (19 vols) which is available for consultation in the reading room of DCLA's Gilbert Library on Pearse Street.

1   Thomas P. Dungan, 'John Dongan of Dublin, an Elizabethan Gentleman', *Journal of the Royal Society of Antiquaries of Ireland*, 118, 1988, 101-17. See also Lena Boylan, *Castletown and its Owners* (Irish Georgian Society, Dublin, 1978); Frederick Van Wyck, *Ancestry of Governor Dongan* (Boston, 1935).

2   Dungan, 'John Dongan of Dublin', 101-17

3   *ibid.*

4   *ibid.,* 114.

5   Van Wyck, *Ancestry of Governor Dongan*, 1-20

6   Boylan, *Castletown and its Owners*, 9.

7   Van Wyck, *Ancestry of Governor Dongan*, 23.

8   Boylan, *Castletown and its Owners*, 11.

9   *ibid.*

10   Thomas Patrick Phelan, *Thomas Dongan, Colonial Governor of New York, 1683-1688* (New York, *c*.1933) 29

11   *ibid.*, 31: 'In 1682 James named Thomas Dongan, Vice-Admiral in the Navy and the first Governor of the Colony of New York, a city of four thousand inhabitants, and eighteen languages.'

12   Peter R. Christoph (ed.), *The Dongan Papers, 1683-1688*, 2 vols (Syracuse, 1993-1996) II, xvi.

13   Donna Merwick, 'Dutch Townsmen and Land Use: a spatial perspective on seventeenth-century Albany, New York', *William and Mary Quarterly*, vol. 37, no. 1, 1980, 73.

14   Phelan, *Thomas Dongan, Colonial Governor of New York*, 134.

15   James Graves, 'Petition of Thomas, Earl of Limerick to Queen Anne for the recovery of property', *Journal of the Kilkenny & South-East Ireland Archaeological Society*, series 2, III, pt. 1, 1860, 9-11. In 1700 Parliament passed the Act of Resumption of the Irish forfeitures, and vested them in trustees before 10th August that year, but due to the loss of his settlement, he could not claim the estate by that act.

16   Graves, 'Petition of Thomas, Earl of Limerick', 9-11.

17   Patrick Walsh and A.P.W. Malcomson, *The Conolly Archive* (Dublin, 2010) 71-72, 13th June 1706[?], Letter from [the Earl of] Limerick (Dublin) to Conolly at his lodgings in Dame Street.

18   Antoine Giacometti and Steve McGlade, 'Archaeological Report, James's and Thomas Street QBC, Dublin 8' (Dublin, 2015) 25.

19   *ibid.*, 52.

20   *ibid.*, 51-54.

21   *ibid.*, 8.

22   DCLA has recently had the map professionally conserved.

23   DCLA, Ancient Revenue 27, Agreement between the Earl of Limerick and Dublin Corporation, dated 20th April 1705, with the accompanying map dated 11th June 1703

24   *ibid.*

25   National Archives, M.6992 (4), Lease from Corporation of Dublin to Thomas Earl of Limerick of Water Course in James's Street, 12th April 1705, between the City and The Right Honorouble Thomas Earle of Limerick.

26   *ibid.*

27   *ibid.*

28   CARD, V (1671-1692), 457-459

29   CARD, VI (1692 to 1715-16), 218-219

30   *ibid.*

31   Irish Architectural Archive, Castletown Papers, E/3/21, 21st September 1709. See Walsh and Malcomson (eds), *The Conolly Archive*, 70: 'Conveyance of Castletown estate from Thomas Dongan, Earl of Limerick to William Conolly'.

32   *ibid.*

33   Christoph (ed.), *The Dongan Papers*, II, no. 2, p.xxiii.

Between the Speaker and the squire: the Anglo-Irish life of William Conolly II

PATRICK WALSH

MAKING HIS WILL IN 1803, THOMAS CONOLLY STIPULATED THAT HIS HEIRS MUST assume the Conolly arms and name and, moreover, that they should be resident in Ireland, 'as their ancestor, Mr Speaker Conolly, the original and honest maker of my fortune, was'.[1] This requirement points to two key themes of the Conolly family history – their dynastic failures and their self-mythologising about their identity as an Irish family. In this desire to perpetuate the family name even in unpromising situations, they were not unique. The late seventeenth and early eighteenth centuries had witnessed a demographic crisis within the British elite leading to increased instances of inheritance by cadet branches of elite families, while the strategy of adopting the family surname by distant relations was frequently deployed to make such transitions more seamless. Emphasising spatial and territorial connections and the obligations these brought was also part and parcel of such elite strategies and allowed continuities to be outwardly presented where the reality of the situation was more complex.[2]

This was undoubtedly true in the case of Edward Michael Pakenham's assumption of the name Conolly to claim inheritance of some of his wife's grand-uncle's estates in 1803. Similar strategies were also central to Thomas Conolly's own attempts to secure his late uncle William Wentworth, 2nd Earl of Strafford's English earldom and Yorkshire estates in the 1790s. Anthony Malcomson has superbly dissected this complex episode in an important essay, which demonstrates the significance of the English connections of Thomas Conolly's mother, Lady Anne Wentworth, to the history of the Conolly family and their fluctuating fortunes, even mischievously arguing that the Conolly marriage alliance with the Strafford family was more significant than Thomas Conolly's marriage into the ducal Richmond family in 1758.[3] This article builds on Malcomson's work but

1 – Rosalba Carriera (1675-1757), WILLIAM CONOLLY (1706-54)

1727, pastel on paper, 57 x 44.5 cm (© Castletown Foundation)

focuses instead on the first of the English Conollys, the Speaker's nephew and heir William James Conolly of Dunton Basset in Leicestershire. His journey from provincial English obscurity to becoming the heir of Ireland's largest fortune, political interest, and of course most important country house, allows us to gain a greater understanding of this neglected figure in the history of Castletown, one whose life embodied the hybrid and complex identity of a true Anglo-Irishman, equally comfortable (or indeed uncomfortable) on both sides of the Irish Sea. This article moves beyond older and out-dated clichés of 'absenteeism' to explore the complex realities of eighteenth-century British and Irish gentry life.[4] It shows that the Conollys' interests were never entirely insular but were instead at least partly orientated towards Britain from the 1720s onwards, even as they outwardly stressed their Irish patriotism in stone and scarves.[5]

William James Conolly (hereafter William Conolly II)[6] first came to public attention as the Speaker's designated heir in March 1721 when the London press reported his appointment to the Irish sinecure office of Cursitor in Chancery. Newspaper reports described him as a student at Greenwich academy and as a nephew of 'the famous Conolly of Ireland'.[7] His life before that is somewhat obscure. He was born in 1699 the only son of the Speaker's only brother Patrick and his wife Frances Hewett, a younger daughter of a minor Leicestershire gentry family, resident, confusingly, at Great Stretton, a property almost identical in name to the later Conolly property at Stretton in Staffordshire (for which see below).[8] This marriage, like the Speaker's own career, reminds us that the Conolly family background cannot have been as obscure as contemporaries and some later historians have suggested.[9] His parents were resident in Worksop in Nottinghamshire at the time of William's birth, though were living in London in 1705 when Speaker Conolly settled £2,000 upon them 'in consideration of the great love and affection I have for my brother'.[10] Patrick Conolly died in 1713, leaving – as his wife had predeceased him – two orphaned children, William and his elder sister Frances, 'described as a pretty solitary girl' of sixteen.[11]

Following Patrick's death, guardianship of William, but not Frances, was entrusted to the Speaker and his wife Katherine, causing some friction between the Conollys and the Hewett family, who no doubt assumed the much wealthier Conollys would provide for both children.[12] The Conollys, though childless themselves, already had some experience of such a role, having been entrusted with the education and upbringing of the three children of Katherine's late brother General Henry Conyngham, who was killed during the War of Spanish Succession in 1707.[13] Central to their role as guardians was the provision for the young Conynghams of an education suitable to their station in life. Thus Williams, the eldest son, was sent off on a grand tour in 1718 where, rather than developing an appreciation for European culture, he contracted venereal disease, ran through his allowance, and made an unsuitable marriage to a Dutch woman.[14] Meanwhile his younger brother Henry was provided with an officer's commission, allowing him to follow in the military footsteps of his father and grandfather, both distinguished soldiers. Finally, Mary, the Conynghams' only daughter, was found a suitable husband, Francis

*2 – PL Ghezzi, CARICATURE OF
WILLIAM CONOLLY ON THE GRAND TOUR
1727, drawing on paper
(© Castletown Foundation)*

Burton, of Buncraggy, county Clare, and was married at Castletown in 1720.[15] While the Conynghams, especially Williams, were not always appreciative of their Conolly relations, it is clear that William and Katherine took their role as guardians seriously, seeking to provide their charges with the best education, connections and opportunities to prosper in British and Irish elite society.

They may have learnt some lessons from their experience with Williams Conyngham by the time they came to oversee the education of William Conolly II. Indeed, even before Patrick Conolly's death he was being advised by the Speaker and his English friends to move to Nottingham to be near a public school to secure a good education for his children.[16] A suitable education was deemed essential for an elite gentleman in this period, with either attendance at public school, university or another high-status institution increasingly common both as a means to familiarise himself with the classics and as an entry point into the social and political world he would be expected to inhabit in adulthood.[17] Greenwich Academy met these requirements. Although only established in 1712, it was already a fashionable place for the sons of the nobility and gentry to study, while its scholarly credentials were confirmed by the school's close links with Greenwich Observatory.[18] After Greenwich, the young Conolly was 'ordered' by his uncle to attend a riding school, again suggesting the care been taken to give him the accomplishments of a gentleman. He was also advised of the perils of 'keeping bad company' and of the dangers of gambling.[19] The young William then virtually disappears from view following his nomination in absentia to the office of Cursitor in Chancery in 1721, a post that brought with it an income of £200 a year as well as entry into the world of official Dublin, dominated by his uncle. There is, however, one tantalising glimpse of him in 1720 in the only letter which survives from him to his uncle, whose advice he seeks about investing his small inheritance from his parents in the then rising South Sea Company.[20] Sadly the Speaker's response has not survived, but it seems likely from other sources that the younger William, unlike some of his Conolly relations, did not invest his small fortune in the infamous bubble.[21]

Increasingly central to a young man of fortune's education was the Grand Tour. Foreign travel, it was believed, would forward the cultivation of the mind as well as the development of a greater appreciation of the European cultural inheritance that was becoming so important in shaping elite identity in this period. The Grand Tour could also allow the tourist to build up a collection of paintings and sculpture to furnish his country house, and it could be used as an entrée point into elite, even royal, society. Conolly II seems to have had two separate tours, both presumably funded by the Speaker's largesse.

He landed in Leghorn, Italy, in December 1726, and visited Florence and then Rome, where the Italian artist, P.L. Ghezzi sketched his portrait in late spring/early summer (Plate 2). Interestingly the text associated with this drawing described him as 'Monsieur Conolly Irlandese'.[22] It is probable that the pastel portrait by Rosalba Carriera now at Castletown (Plate 1) was also painted at this time, but there is no direct evidence of this, or indeed of any purchases being made specifically for Castletown – then, of course, in the process of being furnished.[23] In October 1727 he was reported to be just back from his 'foreign travels' when he was presented at court to the new king, George II, by the Duke of Grafton, himself formerly a close associate and supporter of Speaker Conolly. Conolly II's presentation at court indicates not only that his education and travels had succeeded in polishing the boy from Dunton Bassett, but also that he, and more importantly, his uncle, 'the great Conolly of Ireland', were held in high esteem within elite circles in Britain, an especially impressive feat considering that the elder Conolly had never himself been out of Ireland except for a brief and enforced absence during the tumultuous period of the Glorious Revolution in 1688-89.[24]

It is possible that Conolly II's travels were interrupted by the accession of the new king and by the calling of a parliamentary election in Ireland. This electoral contest gave Speaker Conolly the opportunity to return the younger William as MP for the Conolly's ancestral hometown of Ballyshannon (pictured in the background of his portrait by Anthony Lee (Plate 3), allowing him to begin his political education in the Irish parliament, where he was joined by the two Conyngham brothers, both newly elected for the neighbouring constituency of Killybegs.[25] Following the end of his first parliamentary session, Conolly returned to the Continent to continue his travels, which this time took him to Hanover and then on to Italy by way of Dijon.[26] His trip to Hanover, like his earlier presentation to George II, was intended to give him an entrée to the royal court, this time to that of the heir-apparent to the throne. But this stratagem misfired, because by the time he arrived, Frederick, Prince of Wales had already departed for London.[27]

Shortly after William Conolly II's return from his grand tour, in October 1729, his uncle, Speaker Conolly, died following sporadic bouts of illness during the preceding year. The younger Conolly now came into his inheritance, or at least part of it. The Speaker's will divided the Conolly estates between his widow, his nephew, and Williams Conyngham. Katherine, his widow, received a life interest in Castletown and the Conollys' Dublin town house in Capel Street, as well as in estates in counties Dublin, Kildare, Meath and Roscommon, and outright ownership of a small estate in Wales. Williams Conyngham, meanwhile, inherited the Conolly estate at Newtown Limavady in county Derry, together with control of its two parliamentary seats, although this must have been small consolation for someone who had hoped, and had been widely tipped, to inherit the entire Conolly fortune.[28] The remainder of the vast family patrimony, including estates in Donegal, Derry, Dublin and Westmeath passed to Conolly II, making him, at a stroke, one of the richest men in Ireland.[29] He was also due to inherit Castletown along with the rest of the Conolly property, with the exception of the Welsh estate, upon

3 – Anthony Lee, PORTRAIT OF WILLIAM CONOLLY, M.P. (1699-54)
c.1727, oil on canvas, 119 x 91cm (detail) (© National Gallery of Ireland, currently on loan to Leinster House)

the eventual death of Katherine, who was already in her 67th year. No-one, not least the younger Conolly, could have expected that she would live into her ninetieth year, thereby delaying his enjoyment of the full benefit of his uncle's fortune. In the immediate term, he was saddled with the responsibility of paying the Speaker's generous legacies to other less fortunate relations out of his portion of the estate.

With great wealth came great responsibility. Conolly II, though still a young man (he was 30 in 1729), was expected to take over the management of the Conolly estates as well as his uncle's political interest in the Irish parliament, though in reality this passed to the Speaker's established parliamentary lieutenants, Marmaduke Coghill and Sir Ralph Gore. It was anticipated that he would remain resident in Ireland, where he was made a member of the Privy Council in succession to his uncle, 'the late memorable patriot', and that he would settle down, but initially he seems to have preferred to 'ramble abroad', leaving the management of estate affairs to his uncle Thomas Pearson, the husband of the Speaker's sister Jane.[30] During the 1730 summer season, Conolly II was the toast of Tunbridge Wells, with one woman writing longingly, 'We all desire to marry Mr Conolly'.[31] His departure for Ireland, or that 'wretched country', was much lamented, with one anonymous poet bemoaning the loss of 'so much excellence'.[32] This reaction, if rather overblown, suggests the young Anglo-Irishman had made an impression. He was similarly active on the London social scene in the summers of 1731 and 1732, hunting with the Royal Family, attending balls, and promenading with other young men and women at court.[33] It is notable that his associates in England included few other members of the Irish upper class, suggesting both the ease with which he entered the English elite and his lack of familiarity with the established Irish interest at court.[34]

This rambling spendthrift lifestyle disappointed his Conolly relations. In April 1732 his uncle Thomas Pearson reported a conversation with Conolly about the latter's marriage intentions, writing that 'though he tells me he now designs it, yet I fear his thoughts are more intent upon rambling'.[35] Pearson further declared that he had stipulated that Conolly's future place of residence must be in Ireland. It is unclear how Conolly reacted to this conversation, but by November 1732 he had proposed to Lady Anne Wentworth, the eldest daughter of the Earl of Strafford, whom he had met in London. Six months later they were celebrating their marriage at Strafford's London house in St James's Square.[36]

Conolly's marriage to Lady Anne brought him further into the orbit of the English aristocracy. A god-daughter of Queen Anne, she was the daughter of Thomas Wentworth 1st Earl of Strafford (of the second creation), the head of a famous (or perhaps infamous) family. He was a grandnephew of Thomas Wentworth, 1st Earl of Strafford (of the first creation), Charles I's controversial Lord Deputy of Ireland, who had been executed at the beginning of the English Civil War. Lord Strafford, Lady Anne's father, had spent some of his youth 'wenching and wining' in Dublin while a Trinity undergraduate, before becoming a distinguished soldier and diplomat, through which service he regained the family earldom in 1711, but not the family estates, which had descended to his cousin,

Lord Rockingham.[37] Shortly afterwards, following the death of his patron, the Tory Queen Anne in 1714, his public career came to an abrupt end, and he devoted the remainder of his life to building a country house in the German-Baroque style on his estate at Staineborough in Yorkshire, which he later renamed Wentworth Castle. The degree to which his aesthetic sensibilities, clearly in evidence at Wentworth Castle and his improvements in the landscape there, influenced his daughter and son-in law's contribution to Castletown remains difficult to prove. Strafford's fall from grace, from a position where he and his socially ambitious wife were successfully negotiating their entry into London's 'beau monde' to his genteel retirement to his Yorkshire estates, may have made the marriage of his eldest daughter to an arriviste Irish commoner more acceptable than it would otherwise have been. Indeed, there is some evidence to suggest that Conolly was not the first Irishman who had been under consideration as a possible match for Lady Anne.[38] Nevertheless, despite the somewhat tainted nature of the Strafford name, thanks to the earl's Jacobite associations it was an advantageous match for the socially ambitious Conolly. It was also, of course, advantageous to Lord Strafford, who was able to provide his daughter with a relatively low marriage portion considering the bride's social status. While Strafford might have benefited initially from his daughter's marriage, her jointure of £3,000 per annum paid throughout her long widowhood up to her death in 1797 was a significant drain on the Conolly finances in later decades.

Despite its importance in the history of the Conolly family's fortune and future, frustratingly little evidence has survived about the reaction of either Katherine or any of Conolly's other Irish relations to the marriage, or, indeed, to the bride. Katherine's brief correspondence with Lord Strafford in 1734 after the birth of William and Anne's first child, a daughter, Catherine, suggests that she recognised him as her social superior, even allowing for the Straffords' travails since 1714 – a reversal in fortune that was precisely in contrast to the rise of the Conollys, who were the great Irish beneficiaries of the Hanoverian succession. Her deferential role in their relationship can be glimpsed in her delighted reaction to Lord Strafford's acceptance of the gift of a print of her late beloved husband, an exchange that also highlights the importance of gift-giving in maintaining familial relationships between people who never or rarely met.[39]

Conolly, for his part, seems to have been delighted with his marriage. In a letter to his new father-in-law he earnestly described his love for his new wife: 'You have made me as completely happy as my wishes could have done in giving me Lady Anne and though this is wrote in the honeymoon I believe I shall be able to say as much in seven years hence...'[40] These lines, written on the morning of his marriage in 1733, were echoed in other gushing letters written during the first years of their relationship, which described his delight when his wife's 'big belly' or pregnancy first became apparent, and then at the births of his first daughter, Catherine, and sons William and Thomas. The first son, much to his parents' and especially Katherine Conolly's distress, died soon after birth.[41] There would be five more daughters born, but all was not entirely rosy within the Conolly household. In December 1738 it was reported in London that their marriage was in trouble, while Dublin gossip suggested that he had been 'presented' with a child three years earlier.[42] The marriage did however survive these trying times, partly because the couple gradually abandoned their rather peripatetic lifestyle involving constant shuttling back and forth across the Irish Sea.[43]

This lifestyle had been in many ways an inevitable consequence of Conolly's marriage, which brought with it new opportunities in England to add to his Irish responsibilities. Most obviously his connection with Lord Strafford allowed him to enter the Westminster parliament as an MP for Aldeburgh in Suffolk, the Strafford family borough. Strafford facilitated this election despite their diametrically opposed political views. Conolly described himself as 'an incorrigible Whig', and he quickly became known as a reliable supporter of Sir Robert Walpole's administration in London.[44] His father-in-law, meanwhile, as a Tory with Jacobite sympathies – he had been involved in the 1722 Atterbury plot which sought to implement regime change in Britain and Ireland – was a constant if lonely opposition voice in the House of Lords. Conolly would remain an MP at Westminster until his death, sitting first for Aldeburgh and then, from 1747, for Petersfield in Hampshire, thus initiating a Conolly association with the Westminster parliament which would survive intermittently into the late twentieth century.[46]

Conolly's parliamentary career at both Westminster and College Green was rather undistinguished, especially perhaps when compared to that of either his uncle or, indeed, his son, the often unfairly derided Thomas Conolly.[47] He was a consistent supporter of government, and indeed earned some opprobrium in Ireland for not adhering to the patriot principles of his late uncle. In London, at least, it was the associated social scene that most attracted the Conollys during parliamentary sessions. They were regularly present at court and were sufficiently well known for regular rumours to circulate that Conolly was to be ennobled either as Lord Aldeburgh, Lord Stretton (his English seat) or even Lord Castletown.[48] Such rumours of advancement in the peerage came to nothing, although this was a reflection more on the virtually closed nature of the peerage during the reign of George II than of Conolly's lack of the requisite qualifications.[49] Such rumours do indicate that the Conollys were increasingly orientating themselves towards England, and their frequent appearances on that side of the Irish Sea over a period of eleven years suggest there was some truth in them.

The Conollys' orientation towards England had been apparent since 1733 when, on the eve of his marriage, Conolly purchased an English country house and estate at Stretton in Staffordshire (Plate 4). Purchased for £15,000 from the indebted Congreve family, it provided the newly wedded Conollys with an English base conveniently located on the road to Ireland.[50] The best description of the house comes from one of Lady Louisa Conolly's letters, where she describes her first impressions of the early eighteenth-century seven-bay, two-storey house to her sister, Emily, Countess of Kildare: it 'is really a sweet dear, lovely, pretty place as ever was. The house is charming comfortable.' Going on to describe the interior, she explains how, in addition to four 'very good bedchambers ... to put anybody in', there was 'a green damask drawing room, where there is just such

4 – Anon., STRETTON HALL
c. 1760-90, watercolour (detail) (© William Salt Library, Stafford, Staffs)

a bookcase as one of them at Castletown'. Meanwhile, on the ground floor there was a 'very good hall', a wainscoted dressing room for Mr Conolly and a wainscoted drawing room, as well as a 'pretty India-paper drawing room that looks to the garden'.[51] This decorative scheme is partly attributed to Lady Anne, and raises intriguing questions about their influence on Castletown's decorative scheme in the same period, as well as the inspiration for Castletown's later green drawing room. The acquisition of Stretton, together with the leasing of successive London properties in the fashionable West End, was presumably designed to allow the Conollys to cut the figure in English society which had been so fleetingly enjoyed by the Straffords in the early 1710s.[52] It is notable in this regard that when Conolly was first rumoured to be raised to the peerage in autumn 1733, it was to be as Baron Stretton, suggesting that possession of an English property was a prerequisite to achieving such an elevation.[53]

Stretton Hall was not, however, the only country residence purchased by Conolly. In 1731 he bought Leixlip Castle in county Kildare, adding it to the manor and town purchased by his uncle three years earlier.[54] The purchase of Leixlip gave Conolly his own independent establishment in Ireland, while his aunt, Katherine, remained chatelaine of neighbouring Castletown. Its purchase suggested the dual nature of his Anglo-Irish family, and it was where he settled with his new bride soon after their arrival in Ireland in 1733. First it needed some refurbishment. As Conolly informed Lord Strafford, it was not 'without amendment so fit for a family as a single man'.[55] The links between Leixlip and Castletown were confirmed by the commissioning of Joseph Tudor to paint a view of Leixlip in Castletown's grand entrance hall in the 1730s.[56] Tudor's visual representations were complemented by the poetical imaginings of the local rector (and poet), Samuel Shepherd, in his 1739 work, *Leixlip, a Poem*, which describes a walk along the river Liffey with Conolly, which concludes at 'the gay pile' Castletown.[57] It was at Leixlip that

Lady Anne gave birth to her Irish-born children, including their eventual heir, Thomas Conolly, born there in 1738. Leixlip was the newly arrived Conollys' first home, though we know very little about their work there, or indeed about Lady Anne's initial impressions of her Irish castle.

We do however know something of her initial impression of the other Conolly houses. Coming from the 'palatial splendour' of her father's Wentworth Castle, the young Lady Anne was not overly enamoured with Castletown. She described it to her father thus:

> As to Castletown it is very unfinished without doors. I don't think the place very pleasant, though the house is really a charming one to live in. The front is quite without ornament of any sort, not even so much as a pediment over the windows, and the offices are separated from it by very handsome colonnades, that altogether it looks very well. At least here it does, where there is but few places that are anyway like a seat and so they have all one fault and that is the want of trees, by which reason every place looks horrible raw and cold.[58]

The undecorated façade compared unfavourably with the ornamented pediments and pilasters visible at Wentworth Castle, while the lack of landscaping was in contrast to her father's contemporary improvements in Yorkshire, which included an obelisk devoted to the memory of his patron, and Lady Anne's godmother, the late Queen Anne.[59] Her description of Castletown echoed that of another astute contemporary English visitor, Mrs Delany, who, likewise, commented upon its plain style: 'It is a large heavy building, a vast deal of room in it, but not laid out with a good taste, the furniture good, but not disposed to the best advantage, the situation very fine, and the country about extremely pleasant, some wood and pretty winding rivers.'[60]

Their views warn us that Castletown in its original incarnation was not necessarily the 'ornament to the country' envisaged by Speaker Conolly in the 1720s. Indeed, Lady Anne much preferred another Conolly property, Rathfarnham Castle, in south county Dublin, which she praised rather fulsomely:

> I was a little while ago to see Rathfarnham, which is a place I own I think the best of any I have seen in this country, the house is an old castle with square towers of each corner and has much the air of an English nobleman's seat the gardens are neat and pretty and the park is vastly well wooded ... it is really a sweet place and though not so grand, yet in my mind is more agreeable than Castletown.[61]

Lady Anne's letters to her father betray a certain sense of wistful isolation. This is not surprising as she was a young woman in a foreign country, living with a husband who was not quite a stranger there, though not quite a native either. They did, however, enjoy excellent relations with Katherine Conolly, dining regularly with her at Castletown, while the presence of other Wentworth relations, including Lord Strafford's sister Mrs Donnellan, in Dublin gave Lady Anne a further entrée into the upper echelons of Irish society.[62] However, the strength of both Conollys' desire to return to London can be gauged from their surviving correspondence. In August 1734, for instance, only a year after her arrival in Dublin, Lady Anne told her father: 'My living absent from my friends is to be sure not what I should choose but as I know it is Mr Conolly's affairs not his inclination that keeps him here, it would be monstrous in me to be dissatisfied at it.'[63]

Further hints in Lady Anne's correspondence suggest that her husband found it difficult to adjust to the different style and mode of Irish politics, not least its hard-drinking, convivial elements. On one occasion she mentions how 'His head has not been enough settled to do anything, for drinking as you know does not agree with him, he must practice it a little at his first coming into the country or he would not please.'[64] Conolly was not alone amongst English-based politicians in finding the Dublin parliamentary drinking culture difficult to adjust to; the Earl of Orrery made similar complaints in the mid-1730s. As James Kelly reminds us, alcohol often played a central role in the sociable practice of politics in this period,[65] and in other, more important respects, too, Conolly II failed to live up to the perhaps impossible expectations placed on his shoulders that he would inherit his uncle's political role in Ireland. While possessing the Conolly fortune, he lacked the attention to detail necessary to cultivate an electoral following, leaving Katherine Conolly to continue to deal with the minutiae of Donegal and Londonderry politics.[66] She also continued to act as a political hostess in her own right at Castletown, utilising the house in the ways in which the speaker intended but rarely fully managed himself.[67] Conolly II also lacked the advantages of high office, with its access to deep wells of patronage, which had been so essential to the elder Conolly's success as a parliamentary manager. Finally, he seems not to have inherited the political guile and cunning that characterised the Speaker's political actions in the Irish parliament. What little we know of his personality suggests that he was 'a kind sober young man' best known for his philanthropic activities, whether as a builder of roads at Rathfarnham, supporter of Dr Steevens' Hospital, or as a distributor of famine relief in counties Kildare and Donegal, and for his good manners rather than his skill as a political operator.[68]

This failure to follow in his uncle's footsteps was a source of disappointment to his relations and to others who hoped Conolly II would assume the leadership of the former Conolly party in parliament. An anonymous but well informed account of the Irish political scene in the 1730s described him thus: 'Young Conolly, who inherited the speaker's great estate, was seldom upon the spot, and when he did appear, drew to him respect rather for his private qualities than for his political capacity: his politics seeming to centre in profound submission to the government.'[69]

So concerned was Katherine about this situation that she took the unusual step of writing to an old friend in Whitehall, seeking his intercession with the prime minister, Sir Robert Walpole, to get Conolly II appointed to the Irish revenue board, a body her late husband had once dominated.[70] Her letter not only stressed her nephew's qualities, which included not only his landed and political interest in Ireland, but also his status as an 'Englishman by birth and education'. This latter description may have been intended as a strategy to curry favour with the pro-English policy then favoured by the British ministers when making appointments in Ireland, but it also reflected the reality of her nephew's dual position.[71] In the end her influence failed to ensure Conolly II's appointment, and he instead spent even more time living in England, where he attended the Westminster parliament, voting regularly for the government but serving without great distinction. Occasionally he seems to have been considered useful by the government there as a representative of metropolitan policy in Ireland thanks largely to his good personal relationships with key political figures, including the Lord Lieutenant of Ireland, the 3rd Duke of Devonshire, who stayed at Castletown in early 1738 as Conolly's guest (his son, the 4th Duke – and Lord Lieutenant 1755-57 – would later rent the house in the mid-1750s after Conolly's death) and the future prime minister, Henry Pelham.[72] Indeed, Conolly was expected to play a key role in defending the administration during the controversial Money Bill Crisis of 1753, but his final illness deprived the government of his support in the Commons, much to their disappointment.[73] His intended behaviour during this key political and constitutional crisis can be contrasted with that of his uncle, who, while a loyal government supporter, knew when and how to distance himself from unpopular measures, such as the introduction of Wood's Halfpence in the mid-1720s.[74] In the end, circumstances conspired to save the younger Conolly from betraying his 'patriot' tradition, although it is also probable that the government in London had overestimated his influence in the Irish parliament.

While Conolly II's Irish political career never took off, it is clear that he paid more attention to his other inherited responsibilities on this side of the Irish Sea. His concern for his tenantry during the harsh winters of 1739-40 is well attested to, and it is revealing that he caught the cold that ultimately killed him while out on his farm in the Dublin Mountains (presumably near Rathfarnham) in 1753.[75] His forced inactivity through illness during this politically turbulent year was even more unfortunate on a personal level, as it was only in mid-1752, with the death of the venerable Katherine, then in her 92nd year, that he succeeded to his full inheritance and its attendant revenues. Illness and his untimely death deprived him of the opportunity to enjoy his tenure as master of Castletown, and his intentions for the house and indeed for his personal and political future whether in Ireland or England must, of necessity, remain obscure.

Certainly his widow was not anxious to prolong her time at Castletown. Together with six of her seven children she returned to England. The only child to remain in Ireland was the eldest daughter, Catherine, who shortly after her father's death married Sir Ralph Gore, 6th Baronet, later Earl of Ross. The others, including the Conollys' only son, Thomas, who was then still a schoolboy at Westminster, departed from Castletown, leaving it to be let to a succession of tenants until he came of age and returned from his grand tour.[76] Upon leaving Castletown, Lady Anne might have pondered the fate of another great house in Kildare, which like Castletown had been built to impress.

Jigginstown, near Naas, had been built by her ancestor Lord Deputy Strafford in the 1630s, and had remained unfinished following his execution. In 1734 Lady Anne had told her father of her desire to visit it to pay homage to her illustrious if flawed ancestor, whose portrait after Van Dyck was hung at Castletown during this period.[77] We do not know if she did visit Jigginstown, but she was certainly aware of the fragility of such seemingly enduring structures. Castletown, upon her husband's premature death, like Jigginstown upon Wentworth's, faced an uncertain future. His career and connections had opened to the Conollys prospects and ambitions beyond Ireland; it remained to be seen in 1754 whether his children would prosper in the land of his birth or in the land of his inheritance. As it turned out, his only son, Thomas, married the daughter of an English duke. Together they restored the fortunes of Castletown, while simultaneously maintaining a dual Anglo-Irish identity, which in time led to Thomas Conolly's unsuccessful pursuit of the Strafford earldom upon the death of his Wentworth uncle – a pursuit which demonstrated the durability of that earlier English connection. Two more of his daughters married into Irish families (with mixed results), while the remaining three married into significant English families, thus extending the integration of the Conollys into elite British society.[78] Their advance into the upper echelons of English society were aided by the generous marriage portions (£8,000 each) provided for them in Conolly II's will, although these took a very long time to be paid out, and together with other (overly?) generous provisions of Conolly II's 1733 marriage settlement contributed in no small part to the late eighteenth- and nineteenth-century diminution of the Conolly estates, including the sale of Stretton Hall in 1787. These stories and the complicated disputes over the family inheritances in Ireland and Yorkshire have been chronicled elsewhere, but they too demonstrate the complex dual Irish and English identities of the Speaker's successors. These competing identities, symbolised by his purchase of the houses at Leixlip and Stretton, were the legacy of William Conolly II.

———

ACKNOWLEDGEMENTS

I am grateful to Anthony Malcomson, Jeanne Meldon and Christopher Moore for reading earlier drafts of this paper and for their very useful suggestions and encouragements. Thanks, too, to the Castletown Foundation, and Patrick, 7th Lord Conolly-Carew for the opportunity to consult manuscript materials in their possession.

ENDNOTES

The following abbreviations are used:

BL	British Library	OPW-MU	OPW-Maynooth University Archive and Research Centre at Castletown
IAA	Irish Architectural Archive	PRONI	Public Record Office of N. Ireland
NLI	National Library of Ireland	TCD	Trinity College Dublin

[1] National Archives of Ireland, T17412, Will of Thomas Conolly, 27th May 1799.
[2] James M. Rosenheim, *The Emergence of a Ruling Order: English landed society, 1650-1750* (London, 1998) 14-19: 19.

3 A.P.W. Malcomson, 'The fall of the house of Conolly 1758-1803', in Allan Blackstock and Eoin Magennis (eds), *Politics and Political Culture in Britain and Ireland, 1750-1850: essays in tribute to Peter Jupp* (Belfast, 2007).

4 This literature had its origins in Thomas Prior's famous 1729 *List of Absentees*, which estimated Conolly II's absentee fortune at £1,000. The most important revisionist work on absenteeism is A.P.W. Malcomson, 'Absenteeism in Eighteenth-Century Ireland', *Irish Economic and Social History*, I, no. 1, 1974, 15-35. See also Toby Barnard, 'The Irish in London and The London Irish, ca.1660-1780', *Eighteenth-Century Life*, 39, no.1, 2015, 14-40:18-22.

5 A particular kind of patriotism was central to the ways in which the death of Speaker Conolly was marked. See Patrick Walsh, 'Politics, Patriotism, and Posterity: The funeral of William Conolly in 1729', in Lisa Marie Griffith and Ciaran Wallace (eds), *Grave Matters: death and dying in Dublin 1500 to the present* (Dublin, 2016) 115-28. Linen scarves of Irish manufacture were famously distributed to mourners at Speaker Conolly's funeral, helping initiate a custom designed to boost the local economy.

6 He is often referred to as William Conolly junior but this is both anachronistic and inaccurate as he was not the Speaker's son.

7 *Daily Post* (London), 27th March 1721.

8 On Conolly's place and date of birth, which contradicts other published sources, see OPW-MU, Conolly Papers, uncatalogued MS, Thomas Seagrave to William Conolly, 8th February 1714, and William Conolly II to William Conolly, 30th August 1720, where he anticipates his coming of age at 21 during the following November. On the Hewetts of Great Stretton, see J. Nichols, *The History and Antiquities of the County of Leicester*, 4 vols (1795-1811) II, 581.

9 On the Conolly family's origins, see Patrick Walsh, *The Making of the Irish Protestant Ascendancy: the life of William Conolly, 1662-1729* (Woodbridge, 2010) 11-16.

10 IAA, Castletown Papers, 97/84, G/4/1, Settlement by William Conolly of £2,000 upon his brother Patrick, 1705.

11 OPW-MU, Conolly Papers, uncatalogued MS, Thomas Seagrave to William Conolly, 4th November 1713.

12 *Ibid*. Penelope Hewett to Thomas Seagrave, 3rd November 1713, enclosed in Seagrave to Conolly, 6th November 1713. TCD, Conolly Papers, Ms 3974/2A-D, William Conolly to Rev. [Seagrave] 13th and 15th April, 6th and 20th September 1714. Interestingly Frances Conolly was one of the very few Conolly relations not provided for in Speaker Conolly's will. She married a London merchant, William Rewse, and died in 1733. Frederick Teague Cansick, *A collection of curious and interesting epitaphs copied from the extant monuments of distinguished and noted characters in the cemeteries and church of St Pancras, Middlesex* (London, 1872) 226.

13 Toby Barnard, 'A tale of three sisters: Katherine Conolly of Castletown', in idem, *Irish Protestant Ascents and Descents, 1641-1770* (Dublin, 2004) 266-89: 276-77.

14 NLI, Smyth of Barbavilla Papers, MS 41,579/1, Adamina Wilhelmina Conyngham to Jane Bonnell, 18th April 1718; Williams Conyngham to Conolly, 18th April 1718.

15 For Henry Conyngham, see his entry in Edith Johnston-Liik, *History of the Irish Parliament*, 6 vols (Belfast, 2002) III, 483, while for Mary Burton's wedding see Henry Downes to William Nicholson, 2 June 1720, in John Nichols (ed.), *Letters on various subjects literary, political, and ecclesiastical, to and from William Nicholson, D.D., successively Bishop of Carlisle, and of Derry; and Archbishop of Cashel...*, 2 vols (London, 1809) II, 522-25.

16 OPW-MU, Conolly Papers, uncatalogued MS, Patrick Conolly to William Conolly, 23rd May 1713, see also Thomas Seagrave to William Conolly, 4th November 1713.

17 Rosenheim, *The Emergence of a Ruling Order*, 35-39.

[18] H.D. Turner, *The Cradle of the Navy: the story of the Royal Hospital School at Greenwich and at Holbrook, 1694-1988* (York, 1990) 5.

[19] OPW-MU, Conolly Papers, uncatalogued MS, William Conolly II to William Conolly, 2nd March 1721.

[20] *ibid.*, William Conolly II to William Conolly, 30th August 1720.

[21] East Sussex Record Office, Frewen Family of Brickwall Papers, MS 8283, Assignment of Mortgage of 460 from William Conolly to William Rewse and Frances Rewse (née Conolly), 12th April 1721; Patrick Walsh, *The South Sea Bubble and Ireland: Money, banking and investment, 1690-1721* (Woodbridge, 2014) 99-101.

[22] John Ingamells, *A Dictionary of British and Irish Travellers in Italy, 1701-1800* (Yale, 1997) 234.

[23] S.R. Drumm, 'The Irish patrons of Rosalba Carriera (1675-1757)', *Irish Architectural and Decorative Studies*, VI, 2003, 202-25. I am indebted to Anthony Malcomson for discussions about the provenance of this portrait previously thought to have been of the Duke of Richmond, Lady Louisa's father.

[24] *Daily Post*, 11th October 1727. For a rather pejorative commentary on the elder Conolly's lack of personal familiarity with London, see Jonathan Swift to John Gay and the Duchess of Queensbury, 28th August 1731 in David Woolley, (ed.) *The Correspondence of Jonathan Swift, D.D.*, 4 vols (Frankfurt, 2003) III, 427-28.

[25] Walsh, *The Making of the Irish Protestant Ascendancy*, 22.

[26] *Daily Post*, 21st June 1728.

[27] National Archives (UK), Irish State Papers, SP 63/389/179, 183, Katherine Conolly to Charles Delafaye, 3rd and 6th December 1728.

[28] When he was presented at court in 1719, George I had enquired whether he would inherit his 'uncle's fortune', Polly Molesworth to John Molesworth, 1st December 1719, in *Historical Manuscript Commission – Various Collections* (London, 1913), viii, 282.

[29] National Archives of Ireland, T92, Will of William Conolly, 18th October 1729.

[30] *Universal Patriot*, 17 Feb. 1730; NLI, Smyth of Barbavilla papers, Ms 41,580/24, Thomas Pearson to Jane Bonnell, 16 Mar. 1730.

[31] Miss Chamber to Miss Howard, 27th July 1730 in John Wilson Croker (ed.), *Letters to and from Henrietta, countess of Suffolk, and her second husband, the Hon. George Berkeley: from 1712 to 1767* (London, 1824) 374. See also *Daily Post*, 10th August 1730 where Conolly is listed alongside three duchesses and two earls amongst the persons of distinction at Tunbridge Wells.

[32] Anon., *Tunbridgialia or Tunbridge miscellanies for the year 1730* (London, 1730) 12.

[33] *London Evening Post*, 27th March 1731 and 3rd August 1732. William Wentworth to Ld Strafford, 25th May 1730, same to same, 27th May 1731, in J.J. Cartwright (ed), *The Wentworth Papers, 1705-39* (London, 1883) 461, 463.

[34] On this 'Irish interest', see Barnard, 'The Irish in London', 18-20.

[35] NLI, MS 41,580/24, Thomas Pearson to Jane Bonnell, 27th April 1732. For Speaker Conolly's similar concerns about Williams Conyngham spending his time and fortune in England in the 1720s, see Walsh, *The Making of the Irish Protestant Ascendancy*, 19.

[36] *London Evening Post*, 24th April 1733; *Universal Spectator*, 28 April 1733.

[37] J.N.P. Watson, *Marlborough's Shadow: the life of the first Earl Cadogan* (Barnsley, 2003) 3; L.&M. Frey, 'Thomas Wentworth, 1st earl of Strafford', *Oxford Dictionary of National Biography*, http://www.oxforddnb.com (accessed 15.6.2017).

[38] On the newly ennobled Strafford's aggressive pursuit of status in fashionable London society, see Hannah Greig, T*he Beau Monde: fashionable society in Georgian London* (Oxford, 2013) esp. 36-40. There are some similarities in the way they were judged by contemporaries with the treatment of

the Conollys in polite Dublin society. On the latter, see Walsh, *The Making of the Irish Protestant Ascendancy*, 12-15. For Lady Anne's first Irish fiancé, Matthew Montgomery, who died tragically from a fall from a horse, see Jennifer Downey, 'Unlocking the history of Castletown house through the Conolly portraits', diploma thesis, Institute of Professional Auctioneers and Valuers, 2016, 22.

39 BL, Wentworth Papers, Add Ms 22,228, f.170, Katherine Conolly to Lord Strafford, 28th February 1734. See also BL, Add MS 22,228, f.102, Anne Conolly to Lord Strafford, 29th January 1734.

40 BL, Add MS 22,228, f.77, William Conolly to Lord Strafford, 2nd May 1733.

41 BL, Add MS 22,228, ff.85, 87, 104 and 108, Conolly to Strafford, 18th October and 24th December 1733, 3rd and 23rd February 1734; Katherine Conolly to Jane Bonnell, 9th December 1734; same to same, 14th November 1737, in Gayle Ashford and Mary-Lou Jennings (eds), *The Letters of Katherine Conolly* (forthcoming Dublin, 2018).

42 Historical Manuscripts Commission, *Diary of John Viscount Perceval, first earl of Egmont*, 3 vols (London, 1920) II, 518, entry for 22nd December 1738. Marmaduke Coghill to Edward Southwell, 11th November 1735 in D.W. Hayton (ed.), *Letters of Marmaduke Coghill, 1722-38* (Dublin, 2005) 175.

43 This endless movement can be tracked through contemporary newspapers, which reported by name those passengers on the Dublin yacht they deemed worthy of their readers' attention. See for example *Daily Advertiser*, 10th July 1731 and 29th July 1732, St *James' Evening Post*, 26th May 1733, *Daily Journal*, 26th June 1735, and *Daily Gazeteer*, 9th January 1736.

44 Quoted in Romney Sedgwick, 'Conolly, William', in *idem* (ed.), *History of Parliament, 1715-54*, available at www.historyofparliamentonline.org (last accessed 15.6.2017).

45 Linda Colley, *In Defiance of Oligarchy: the Tory Party, 1714-60* (Oxford, 1982) 188, 198.

46 Patrick, 7th Baron Conolly-Carew sat in the House of Lords until the abolition of the hereditary seats in the Lords, while successive Conollys represented County Donegal in the union parliament from the 1820s through to the 1870s.

47 See Malcomson 'Fall of the house of Conolly'.

48 *London Evening Post*, 6th September 1733; *Daily Post Boy*, 25th April 1735; *General Evening Post*, 20th September 1735; *London Evening Post*, 14th October 1735; *The Craftsman*, 14th October 1735; *London Daily Post*, 8th October 1739; and *London Evening Post*, 28th January 1744.

49 John Cannon, *Aristocratic Century: the peerage of eighteenth-century England* (Cambridge, 1984) 19-26. It should be noted that Henry Bromley, one of those whose names were regularly mentioned in dispatches as likely to be raised in the peerage alongside Conolly, was created Baron Montfort in 1741 thanks to a bribe paid to the King's mistress, Lady Yarmouth, *ibid.*, 25.

50 For details of the purchase of Stretton Hall, see TCD, Conolly MS 3794/17-28, 10th July 1732 – 20th July 1734. Conolly later added further property to the Stretton estate, *London Daily Post*, 18th November 1738.

51 Lady Louisa Conolly to Emily, Countess of Kildare, 1 March 1759 in Brian FitzGerald (ed.), *Correspondence of Emily, Duchess of Leinster, 1731-1814*, 3 vols (Dublin, 1949-57) III, 2-3. Unfortunately Stretton was remodelled in the late eighteenth century, removing most traces of the Conolly occupancy of the house.

52 On Stretton, see Nikolaus Pevsner, *The Buildings of England: Staffordshire* (London, 1974) 271. On the Straffords' attempts to penetrate the beau monde, the informal elite of London society, see Greig, *The Beau Monde*.

53 *London Evening Post*, 6 September 1733.

54 IAA, Castletown Papers, E16/15, Bond of agreement between William Conolly and John Whyte, 7th August 1731, for the purchase of Leixlip Castle for £1,770.

55 BL, Add MS 22,228, f.81, Conolly to Ld Strafford, 12th September 1733.

[56] Anne Crookshank and the Knight of Glin, 'Note on a newly discovered landscape by Joseph Tudor', *Studies*, 65, 1976, 235-38.

[57] Samuel Shepherd, *Leixlip, A Poem* (Dublin, 1739) 12.

[58] BL, Add MS 22,228, f.89, Anne Conolly to Ld Strafford, 3rd November 1733.

[59] *ibid.*, Pevsner Architectural Guides, *The Buildings of England: Yorkshire the West Riding* (2nd ed., London 1967) 546-48.

[60] Lady Llanover (ed.), *Autobiography of Mary Granville, Mrs Delany...*, 6 vols (London, 1861) I, 343.

[61] BL, Add MS 22,228, ff.120-21, Anne Conolly to Ld Strafford, 5th May 1734.

[62] Katherine Conolly to Jane Bonnell, 28th May 1734, in Ashford and Jennings (eds), *The Letters of Katherine Conolly*; BL, Add MS 22,228 ff.89-91, Anne Conolly to Lord Strafford, 3rd November, 2nd December 1733.

[63] *ibid.*, f.134, Anne Conolly to Lord Strafford, 17th August 1734.

[64] *ibid.*, f.120-21, Anne Conolly to Lord Strafford, 5th May 1734.

[65] James Kelly, 'The consumption and sociable use of alcohol in eighteenth-century Ireland', *Proceedings of the Royal Irish Academy, Section C: archaeology, Celtic studies, history, linguistics, literature, vol. 115C, food and drink in Ireland*, 2015, 219-55: 246-47.

[66] Katherine Conolly to Jane Bonnell, 6th July 1737 in Ashford and Jennings (eds), *The Letters of Katherine Conolly*.

[67] It may not have been Katherine's intention to overshadow her nephew, but her force of personality seems to have been hard to resist, Barnard, 'A tale of three sisters', 280-83.

[68] *London Evening Post*, 18th January 1735 and 29th September 1737; *London Daily Post*, 22nd January 1740; Shepherd, *Leixlip, A Poem*, 1.

[69] Anon., *Ireland Disgraced: or the Island of Saints become an Island of Sinners Clearly Proved...* (London, 1758).

[70] TCD, Conolly Papers, MS 3794/30, Katherine Conolly to Charles Delafaye 2nd June 1736. It is noteworthy that Conolly's name was not mentioned by other prominent figures when the vacancy at the Board was being discussed, suggesting he was not seriously considered for it. See Patrick McNally and Kenneth Milne (eds), *The Boulter Letters* (Dublin, 2016) 409-10.

[71] On this policy, see Patrick McNally, '"Irish and English interests", national conflict within the Church of Ireland episcopate in the reign of George I', *Irish Historical Studies*, 29, 1995, 295-314.

[72] *Daily Gazetteer*, 5th January 1738. Barnard, 'A tale of three sisters', 282. On Conolly's connection to Pelham, see PRONI, Chatsworth Papers, T3158/250, Pelham to Devonshire, 7th November 1743, and Wilmot Papers, T3019/1231, Bellingham Boyle to Weston, 28th December 1748.

[73] PRONI, Chatsworth Papers, T3019/2182, Lord George Sackville to Henry Pelham, 10th October 1753 and T3019/2012A, Thomas Waite to Robert Wilmot, 3rd January 1754. On the Money Bill crisis, see David Dickson, *New Foundations, Ireland 1660-1800* (Dublin, 2000) 98-100.

[74] Walsh, *The Making of the Irish Protestant Ascendancy*, 173-77.

[75] PRONI, T3019/2197, Sackville to Robert Wilmot, 4th November 1753.

[76] For Thomas Conolly's grand tour, see Malcomson, 'The fall of the house of Conolly', 109, and Conolly-Carew Papers, private collection, accounts of William Conolly's executors with Arnold Nesbit, 3rd July 1755 – 7th July 1758.

[77] BL, Add MS, 22,228, f.120, Anne Conolly to Ld Strafford, 5th May 1734.

[78] The only Conolly marriage to end as an unambiguous disaster was that of Thomas's sister Jane, who married the infamous 'Fighting' George Fitzgerald, a well-known duelist who died on the gallows after a scandalous life.

———

Master of the hounds and 'Father of the Turf': Tom Conolly and his equine exploits

PATRICIA McCARTHY

T HREE YEARS AFTER HIS MARRIAGE TO LADY LOUISA LENNOX, THIRD DAUGHTER OF the 2nd Duke of Richmond in 1758, Thomas Conolly, the wealthy twenty-three-year-old owner of Castletown, county Kildare, took a lease on a house in Kildare town from a local carpenter, Richard Hetherington, to use as a base for his racing interests at the Curragh racecourse in that county.[1] In addition to this house, Conolly maintained stables for his racehorses ('Connollys Stables'), on the perimeter of the Curragh racecourse, which can be seen on an 1807 'Map of the Curragh of Kildare showing The Race Courses Gentlemens Seats &c, surveyed by H. Walker' (Plate 2), a short distance from the town. Close to the stables he rented a couple of fields, together with houses or cottages to accommodate his large staff there, some of whom came from Castletown, others from Kildare town.[2] Also on this map is a straight course called 'Conolly's Mile' (so-called after him), running east to the winning post opposite the stand house.

Described as 'the greatest figure in the history of horse-racing and breeding in eighteenth-century Ireland', Conolly had a passion for horses for both racing and hunting.[3] The caption beneath a framed portrait that hangs in the headquarters of Horse Racing Ireland tells how he 'became the mainstay of the Curragh Jockey Club', leading to the founding of the Turf Club in 1790, which earned him the soubriquet 'Father of the Turf Club'. It goes on to say that he 'raced extensively, donated cups and prizes, paid for the promotion of racing and for a school master and textbooks for jockeys and stable lads' at his Curragh stables.

While Louisa's great attachment to Castletown as a house, a home and a place of hospitality and entertainment has been well documented, this essay will look at Conolly's devotion to the equine activities that took up a great deal of his time and money. Despite

1 – Vaulted stables at Ardbraccan, county Meath, designed by Richard Castle, c.1735
(courtesy Irish Architectural Archive)

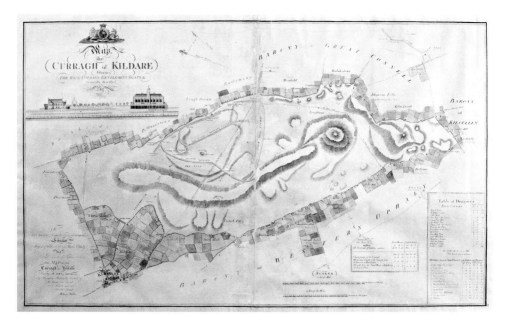

2 – 'Map of the Curragh of Kildare showing The Race Courses Gentlemens Seats &c', surveyed by H. Walker, 1807, showing Kildare town (bottom left) and Conolly's stables on the racecourse
(Courtesy James Adam & Sons)

the suggestion of his 'miserly instincts', it would appear that Louisa had a free rein (no pun intended) at Castletown, where the house became her passion, while her husband pursued his outdoor interests in tandem.[4]

The newly acquired house in Kildare town was described as 'a good dwelling house, pleasure and kitchen garden of 1R[ood], 5P[erches]', and referred to as 'Kildare Lodge'. Louisa lost no time in staying there; on 2nd July 1761 she wrote, 'I was at Kildare for one night with Mrs Clements, she had never been there before. We played at Loo the whole day, I won, she lost', and on 23rd January 1763 she went out hunting with Fanny (Conolly's sister)

> while we were at Kildare, the Curragh is such a charming place for riding that it's mighty pleasant and there is not the least danger, we never attempt leaping. Mr Conolly has a great deal to do there generally for he has now a great many running horses. We had a very pleasant party there...[5]

Another visitor to Kildare town in 1761 was Lord Chief Baron Edward Willes: 'I lay at Kildare wh[ic]h is made a very pretty town by means of the gentle[me]n belonging to the Kildare Hunt. Their number is 61 and most have built for themselves little pretty lodges in the town for the convenience of hunting'.[6] The Lord Lieutenant, the Duke of Rutland (1784-87), was a frequent visitor to Castletown and to Kildare Lodge during his term of office.[7]

It is clear that Conolly's hunters were stabled at Castletown; there are references to that effect in his accounts.[8] From the accounts too, it is evident that the stables at the Curragh were thatched, but little else is known of them.[9] This was a far cry from the stables at Castletown where, in the 1720s, the architect Edward Lovett Pearce designed a range of stables in the east wing as part of the Palladian layout of the house. Here, his seven-bay stable pavilion introduced something that was completely new in stable architecture in Ireland – a vaulted ceiling, supported by Tuscan columns that acted as heelposts for the stalls (Plate 1). This innovative feature, which became a leitmotif for Pearce's assistant, Richard Castle, after Pearce's early death in 1733, was subsequently used at Carton and many other houses.[10] Though they became relatively common in Ireland, vaulting in stables was exceptional even in aristocratic stables in Britain, where it was considered to be too expensive for most owners.[11] But by the beginning of the eighteenth century, stables were becoming important status symbols in Ireland among the nobility and gentry. They were somewhere to take one's guests to view not just the building, but the horses within, which, like works of art, required a deal of connoisseurship in order to appreciate them. There was a difference too in stables that accommodated farm horses and those that accommodated riding and carriage horses, racehorses and hunters. The latter were located closer to the house for the convenience of the family, and were usually of some architectural interest.[12]

The ground-floor plan of Castletown featured in Finola O'Kane's recent essay in

3 – 'Castletown House the Seat of the Rt. Honble Thomas Connolly'
(from the single-volume quarto first edition of Arthur Young's A TOUR IN IRELAND 1776-1779)

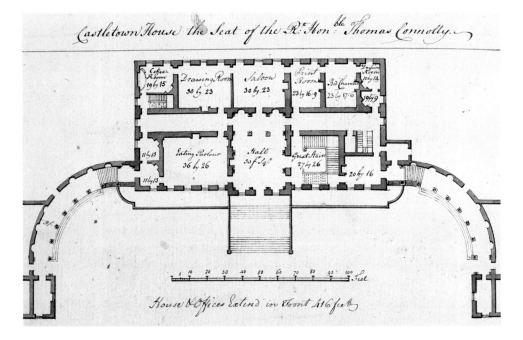

4 – A mounting block in the stable yard at Ardbraccan, Co Meath (photo: the author)

this journal on Arthur Young's 'A Tour of Ireland, 1776-1779' shows how convenient the Palladian plan was for Conolly (Plate 3).[13] His study was located to the front of the house in the two-bay space (20ft x 16ft) from where he could gain access via the colonnade to the stables in the east pavilion.[14] At Ardbraccan, county Meath, where the Palladian lay-out is similar but smaller in scale than at Castletown, a mounting block was erected at the bottom of a flight of steps from the side of the house. There the Bishop of Meath, the house's builder, could mount his horse (Plate 4).

HORSE RACING

THE TITLE 'FATHER OF THE TURF' WAS ONE THAT CONOLLY EARNED. HE WAS A MEM-ber of the Jockey Club from at least 1761, when a receipt for his subscription to the club, a forerunner of the Turf Club, was issued to him.[15] Their clubhouse was the purpose-built (in 1759) Coffee House in Kildare town. With stables at the Curragh and a house leased in the town, as well as Castletown a short distance away, it was no surprise that Conolly played a major part in the Jockey (later Turf) Club.[16] By 1777 it was evident that all was not well within the club: rules were being broken, and in a letter to Conolly in March of that year, the Curragh ranger remarked that 'sporting seems to decline at the Curragh', suggesting that a meeting be called 'for choosing Stewards for the Stand House and Course'.[17] Conolly stepped up to the mark, and under his direction a new code of regulations was drawn up regarding the conduct of races, aimed at improving the regulation of horse racing in Ireland under the auspices of the Jockey Club. At the time his reforms were not successful as the members tended to prioritise the social aspects of membership rather than the regulatory ones, and the club ceased to function in the early 1780s. However, the Turf Club, which came into existence in the 1780s, adopted Conolly's regulations and established itself as the regulating authority of Irish horse-racing.[18]

From the early decades of the eighteenth century, horse-racing was hugely popular in Ireland. An interesting aspect of the sport at that time was the proliferation of the 'my horse against yours' type of race, a match where just two horses were pitted against each other in a test of speed and strength and on which bets were placed.[19] Examples include a four-mile race at the Curragh on 26th April 1763, where Conolly bet 1,000 guineas on his horse, Surly, beating 'Mr Rowley's bay horse Scandenberg', to become 'Horse of the Year', and in 1775 he bet 2,000 guineas that his horse Shoemaker would beat Lord Drogheda's Chestnut Pope, which was the largest eighteenth-century Irish race purse and one that set a record for almost forty years.[20] In the final Jockey Club purse held in April 1781 (before it became the Turf Club purse), Conolly's Smuggler was the winner.[21]

Louisa was justly proud of her husband's successes in horse-racing, and kept her sisters up to date on his prowess. Perhaps she was aware that they did not have the highest opinion of Conolly, describing him as 'immensely silly' and 'tiresome' among other disparaging adjectives.[22] But her pride in this aspect of his life was not misplaced. In 1768 Conolly had nine winners in seventeen races, with winnings amounting to £2,790. His most lucrative winnings were in 1774 and 1775 when he netted £4,823 and £4,928 respectively.[23] According to Tony Sweeney, Conolly set an ownership record 'that stands to this day, namely that he raced nine "Horses of the Year", the best being Tennis-ball'.[24] Another of his horses, The Friar, had a particularly successful 1777 season at the Curragh, and the following year Louisa had the pleasure of seeing her mare Tigress beat The Friar on the same racecourse.[25] From Yorkshire, John Coghill wrote to Conolly in October 1778: 'I sincerely congratulate you on the goodness of your Horses. Your Stable has done more last meeting at the Curragh than any Stable I ever heard of.'[26] This was well-deserved praise for Conolly whose record, according to Sweeney, gives him a career total of 265 winners between 1760 and 1796, and a total of £37,598 in winnings.[27]

Despite his winnings, Conolly's success at the Curragh and elsewhere with his horses, came at a price. There was his predilection for gambling, which will be looked at later. His accounts show that from the 1760s onwards a great deal of money was expended on maintaining his equine interests. He had a large staff at the Curragh stables, as well as his hunting pack, their kennels, and his stables and staff at Castletown. He provided medical care, a schoolmaster, books, board and clothes for the stable boys at the Curragh, who were paid £6 per annum. That the boys were well looked after is evident from the accounts, with regular payments for clothes and shoes, such as, in June 1778, a tailor's bill 'for Clothing 9 boys at the Curragh completely white liveries, fustian frocks &

surtouts £52. 18s 11d' and another 'for 20 pr breeches' for them for £20 8s 4d. In 1784 Henry Lee sent an invoice 'for the making of shoes for the little boys about the stables £2. 8s 7d', and the following year '20 felt hats' were provided for them for £2 14s 2d.[28] John Scott, who was responsible 'for dieting and dressing the stable boys', had another responsibility as 'Feeder in the Stables' (presumably for the horses) and was paid £68 5s per annum. Conolly also personally paid the bill for advertising racing fixtures in Faulkner's *Dublin Journal*. In addition to these expenses he sponsored numerous horse races: he presented a Gold Cup, valued at 200 guineas, for a race to be run at the Curragh. As an extensive landowner in the north-west of Ireland, he also presented a silver cup, valued at £40, and inscribed 'The Right Honorable Thomas Conolly to the City of Derry', for a race between horses owned by the freeholders of Derry.[29] This did him no harm as the Member of Parliament for Londonderry. He also enjoyed and took part in racing with his own horses at Down Royal's fixtures. Before horseboxes, horses were walked to and from race venues. A letter to Conolly in 1779 from his friend Francis Savage, who was looking after his stable arrangements in Down, illustrates this:

> I have this instant been looking at your horses brushed over and am happy in being able to inform you that they are both extremely well after having travelled twenty miles this day, of bad road from Castlewellan hither. Filch is extremely sound and well, his race of yesterday all considered. Early tomorrow they will set forward and reach Enniskillen sooner than Wednesday.[30]

Filch is distinguished in Irish record books as the horse with twenty consecutive victories between 1778 and 1780.[31]

HUNTING

A WRITER IN 1719 OBSERVED OF THE IRISH THAT THEIR 'NOBILITY ARE MUCH GIVEN TO recreations and pastimes as hunting, hawking, riding, drinking, feasting and banqueting with one another'.[32] Fifty years later, not much had changed apart, probably, from 'hawking'. The painting *The Kilruddery Hunt* (1740s) is one of the earliest paintings of a fox-hunt where the Earl of Meath's seat in county Wicklow is the background to cut-outs of hounds, huntsmen, horses and stags that have been pasted onto the surface of the picture. 'The Kilruddery Hunt' is also a song celebrating a hunt in 1744 with the hounds of the 6th Earl of Meath that describes the exploits of leading sportsmen of the area. It was still being sung in playhouses at the end of the century.[33] In the 1820s the 7th earl showed exemplary commitment to the chase by managing to hunt in Kildare during the season while staying at Kilruddery:

> [He kept] his hunters in county Kildare, and having two hacks, one in Dublin and one at Kilruddery, riding into town, changing there, & going to wherever the meet

took place, where his hunter awaited him. The return journey made in the same way and a hard gallop the entire distance. On one occasion they killed near the Hill of Allen, n.e. of the Curragh, and he returned that night in time for dinner as [his parents] were very particular about punctuality.[34]

The Ponsonby family at Bishopscourt, county Kildare, kept a substantial racing establishment, where the frenetic pace of the hunting fraternity was illustrated in a 1726 guest's letter describing his day's activities:

> I went to bed last night at one of ye clock, was on horseback this morning at four, rid eight miles before daybreak, hunted a fox afterwards, came back afterwards here to dinner, and rid a coursing this afternoon till nightfall, and I thank God I cannot say I am much the worse for it.[35]

It was not only the men who had such stamina. Lady Hester Westenra kept her own pack of hounds in county Laois and managed to strike a bargain for her purse when approached by a highwayman during a hunt in the 1740s. Together they raced after the hounds which had just broken covert; after a long run which Hester won with ease, she offered him her purse but the highwayman bowed and graciously refused to take it.[36] Another enthusiast, Hayes St Leger, the 4th Viscount Doneraile kept a hunting journal in which he kept an account of those in which he took part in both Ireland and England. He recorded the route taken, the numbers killed and what horse he rode.[37] He kept a pet fox from which he caught rabies, resulting in his death in France where he had gone in search of a cure from Louis Pasteur.[38]

By 1764 Conolly had acquired his own pack of foxhounds.[39] Breeding of both hounds and horses was important, and strains were imported from England and continental Europe to improve the breeds used. This reflected well on the owner,[40] as hounds were considered heirlooms that were bred carefully for generations.[41] By 1777 Conolly had established a relationship with the Duke of Rutland's Belvoir pack, said to be among the best in England, through which he improved Castletown's. In June of that year, the Duke's agent wrote from Belvoir Castle asking Conolly to 'send your Huntsman to us as soon as possible, as ... one of the best brood bitches, which is allotted for you, will very soon be too big with whelp to travel, and her whelps I am sure will be very valuable'.[42] Later in June, the Duke's agent sent him, 'eleven couple of hounds that I hope will please you', in addition to 'four Bitches from whom we have bred excellent hounds, and also six young Bitches that I daresay will breed you as good'. For Lady Louisa 'with my best respects', he sent a couple of small bitches called Isabell and Lady – 'They will run up with your Hounds and they will breed Large Hounds, being Dwarf Hounds of a Large sort'.[43] A couple of weeks later, in a letter to Conolly, James Agar, Baron Clifden, from Gowran, county Kilkenny, offered 'ten or twelve couples of good running hounds as possibly you can get anywhere'. He had heard that Conolly was 'very low in hounds and that many of your whelps had died', and that as he (Agar) is not in the country much dur-

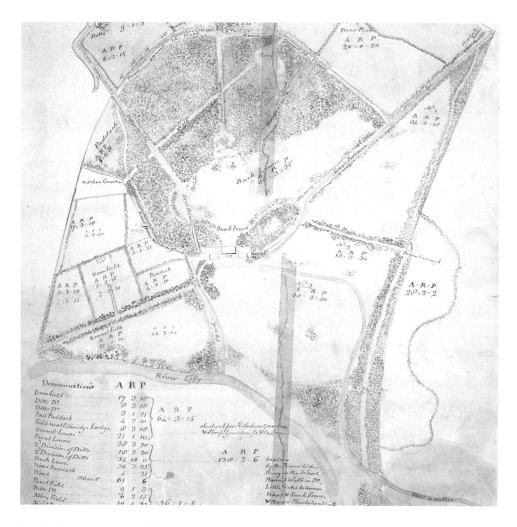

ing the hunting season, it is not worth his while keeping them 'and I know you will keep them up well'.[44]

In an account of his estate since coming of age, Conolly listed the building of dog kennels at Castletown at some time prior to 1773.[45] These were located in the Kennel Field at the Celbridge Gate (Plate 5). Triangular in shape, the field measured over twenty-one acres and was bound by the Liffey to the south and by the main avenue to the north. No image has come to light of the kennels, but from information among the accounts, the exterior walls were pebble-dashed with stone detail, and it had an archway and a pediment to which was attached a pole with the figure of a 'gilded fox' on the top.[46] As a pack of foxhounds was highly bred and expensive to keep, their lodgings required as much thought as those for their equine partners. Built at a height for drainage purposes, they were built of brick, timber or stone with a thatched roof to keep the kennels warm in winter and cool in summer. A drawing by Edward Lovett Pearce shows a 'Dogg house' with a stream of water issuing from an opening in the centre, in which are two lodging rooms (*c*.28ft x 14ft) with benches on which the dogs slept, two other rooms, one perhaps a feeding room, and a boiler house for preparing their food. There is a pitched roof over the centre of the building and a Diocletian window in the gable (Plate 6). Designs for kennels are comparatively rare, and it is doubtful that many would be as extravagant as a design commissioned from John Soane by Frederick Hervey, the Earl Bishop of Derry, in 1779, for Downhill, his house in county Derry, in which three arms extend from a central domed rotunda (where the male dogs were lodged). One arm lodged a keeper, another a heated sick-bay and the third accommodated the bitches. The decoration on the attic of the drum was a canine version of a classical frieze, with heads of dogs replacing ox-heads.[47]

Maintaining a pack of hounds was expensive. Many were purchased in England and someone paid to accompany them to Dublin, and together with board, food, medical expenses, dog collars with engraved brass plates, John Britton was paid £106 7s 6d in August 1780 'for keeping the hounds, the Dog Bog, Firing for the kennels and my own wages [for one year] up to 1 July 1780'.[48] It appears that when there was a shortage or a potential shortage of foxes to hunt, Conolly 'imported' them.[49] In 1778, when there was such a shortage in Kildare, the Conollys took a lodge in Nenagh, county Tipperary, for a month.[50] By the middle of the nineteenth century, private packs, such as his, were replaced by 'subscription packs' that were maintained at communal expense.[51] A 1770s letter, written by Louisa to her husband from her family home at Goodwood in West Sussex,

6 – Edward Lovett Pearce (attrib.), elevation and plan of a 'Dogg House'
(courtesy Irish Architectural Archive)

opposite

5 – Detail of demesne plan of Castletown, c.1768, showing the Kennel Field (bottom left), bounded to the south by the river Liffey, to the north by the Maynooth avenue to the house, and to the east by a pond
(courtesy National Library of Ireland)

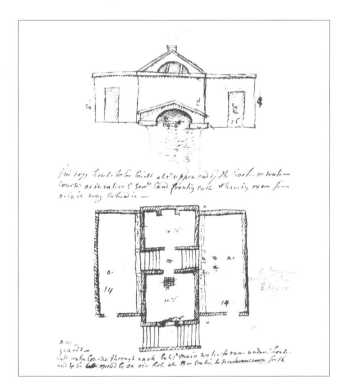

betrayed the couple's second thoughts on maintaining the Castletown pack:

> I do think as you do, that your keeping hounds in Ireland does not answer, and yet as you have so much pleasure in them, 'twould be a 1,000 pities to have you give them up, and that makes me so eager for your having a hunting lodge here, which would answer so well in every respect. It would be an additional expence, but still I think not more than you can well afford, I don't imagine it could be more the differences of 200 a year at most...[52]

Nothing seems to have come of her suggestion, and by the late 1780s, after a bad winter and a bad hunting season, the hounds had to go.[53] In 1814 Louisa (a widow since 1803), was concerned about mending the roof on 'the old Kennels at the Slip near Castletown Gate', and it was on that site that she set up Ireland's first industrial school for boys, where they were taught carpentry, tailoring, shoe-making and basket-making.[54] No trace of Castletown's kennels remains.

Conolly was the first Master of the Castletown Hunt, whose silver buttons were specially made by the goldsmith Jeremiah D'Olier in Dublin, while a Mr Finegan made up the hunt's riding habits. A series of studies painted by Robert Healy in February 1768 records the Conollys and their friends as they hunted and occupied themselves with other outdoor activities at Castletown.[55] All who hunted with Conolly during the day were automatically invited to have supper at Castletown.[56] There he provided a large room in the stables at the east pavilion reserved for his 'guests in boots' – those gentlemen who arrived on horseback too late for supper and who required a meal before an early start the next day.[57] He was the richest commoner in Ireland in the 1750s and his generosity and hospitality were unbounded. In 1778 he sent a present of a horse to his brother-in-law in England, who responded, 'The grey mare came safe and well and is the admiration of the whole country – she has great speed and power to carry my fat wife and I together if occasion.'[58] It may have been a peace offering as, the same brother-in-law, General Sir William Howe, had written to Conolly on his gambling pursuits earlier in the year: 'How goes horses and hounds? I hope with the same success as Almack's from whence I hear you waddled off with £8,000, and I hope never to return where you may be subject to the frowns of Madam Fortune who was so propitious last winter.'[59] His gambling was excessive, and while it worried some, Louisa remained unperturbed. In a letter quoted in Sweeney's book she wrote:

> The dear soul was so often called to Almack's Club in London by bets upon his horses that it drew him into a little gambling. The money he lost won't really hurt him ... It was reported he had ruined himself but I am sure his losses altogether were under £10,000.[60]

Perhaps if his marriage had not been childless he may not have been so incompetent with money. He remarked in 1773 that he had 'no occasion to save money, having no children, and I flatter myself that the money I have spent annually was rationally employed by living, not extravagantly, but like a gentleman.'[61]

Though possessing many good qualities, he had, as Malcomson puts it, serious defects as both a public figure and a business man. He was 'pleasure loving and inattentive to affairs, procrastinating, easily-led and at the same time stubborn, impulsive and not particularly bright', and fundamentally 'ill-suited to manage so great an inheritance and live up to the role that fortune had assigned him'.[62]

EPILOGUE

IN DIFFERENT WAYS TOM AND LOUISA CONOLLY MADE THEIR INDIVIDUAL MARKS ON HIStory – hers in the improvements of both the house and demesne of Castletown, his in his special place as 'Father of the Turf' in Ireland. When Louisa needed advice on matters of architecture and décor, she turned not to her husband, but to her brother-in-law, the Duke of Leinster.[63] Conolly's 'meek' response when she asked his advice on décor in the 1770s was, as she related to her sister Sarah, that 'he thought [she] knew best', which was probably correct.[64] A remark by Louisa's sister Emily, Lady Kildare is telling:'Do you think that I have come to my years without distinguishing between the real and settled wish of spending one's life together, and the hurry of a boy [Conolly?] to come to what he will leave the next half hour for a new hound or horse?'[65] Whatever his shortcomings, there was still, at the turn of the eighteenth century, 'no figure who repeatedly dominated the sport in Ireland in terms of unbroken victories',[66] and no one can take from Tom Conolly his achievements in horse racing, breeding and hunting, nor his generosity in sponsorship and in hospitality.

———

ENDNOTES

The following abbreviations are used:

IAA	Irish Architectural Archive	NAI	National Archives Ireland
JKAS	Journal of the Kildare Archaeological	NLI	National Library of Ireland
	Society	TCD	Trinity College Dublin

[1] Lena Boylan, 'Kildare Lodge, Lord Edward Fitzgerald's House', *JKAS*, XVI, no. 1, 1977-78, 26-35. Hetherington had purchased a lease of thirty-four acres in Kildare town from the Earl of Kildare in 1746. In a 'Statement of his Affairs' since coming of age, Conolly records that he 'bought two lodges, one at the Black Rock, for bathing in the sea, the other at Kildare', for the sum of £1,000. TCD, Conolly Papers, MSS 380-81.

[2] Boylan, 'Kildare Lodge'.

[3] Fergus A. D'Arcy, *Horses, Lords and Racing Men: the Turf Club 1790-1990* (The Turf Club, The Curragh, 1991) 6.

[4] See Finola O'Kane, *Landscape Design in Eighteenth-Century Ireland: mixing foreign trees with the*

natives (Cork University Press, 2004) 118: 'His miserly instincts are suggested in his account books, where Louisa's pin money payments were made consistently late.' TCD MS 3963, Tom Conolly's Personal Account Book, '1766, February 5th, Paid Louisa on account of her Xmas Pin Money: £125.0.0'.

5   Boylan, 'Kildare Lodge'.

6   James Kelly (ed.), *The letters of Lord Chief Baron Edward Willes to the Earl of Warwick 1757-62* (Aberystwyth, 1990) 69.

7   Brian FitzGerald, *Lady Louisa Conolly 1743-1821* (London, 1950) 143.

8   TCD, Conolly Papers, MS 3940/79

9   *ibid.*, MS 3974/252.

10 Vaulted stables designed by Richard Castle can be seen at Gill Hall, county Down, Strokestown House, county Roscommon, Bellinter and Ardbraccan, both in county Meath, Russborough, county Wicklow, in unexcuted plans for Headfort, county Meath, and in plans for Leinster House, Dublin.

11 Giles Worsley, *The British Stable* (Yale, 2004) 149.

12 Patricia McCarthy, 'Stables and Horses in Ireland *c.*1630-1840', *The Provost's House Stables: buildings and environs, Trinity College Dublin* (TRIARC, Dublin, 2008) 28-71.

13 Finola O'Kane, 'Arthur Young's published and unpublished illustrations for 'A Tour of Ireland 1776-1779', *Irish Architectural & Decorative Studies*, XIX, 2016, 118-160.

14 *ibid.*, 132.

15 TCD, Conolly Papers, MS 3974/132.

16 Paul Rouse, *Sport and Ireland, A History* (Oxford University Press, 2015) 67.

17 D'Arcy, *Horses, Lords and Racing Men*, 8.

18 James Kelly, 'The pastime of the elite: clubs and societies and the promotion of horse racing' in Martin J. Powell and James Kelly (eds), *Clubs and Societies in Eighteenth-Century Ireland* (Dublin, 2010) 409-24.

19 James Kelly, *Sport in Ireland 1600-1840* (Dublin, 2014) 70-73.

20 Tony and Annie Sweeney, *The Sweeney Guide to the Irish Turf from 1501 to 2001* (Dublin, 2002) 346-47; Kelly, *Sport in Ireland*, 85, footnote.

21 Sweeney, *The Sweeney Guide*, 17.

22 IAA, Bunbury Letters, 94/84, 1793, from Louisa Conolly to Sarah Bunbury from Castletown, 14th August 1767; Bunbury Letters 94/136, Box 1, from Louisa to same, May 1768; Brian FitzGerald (ed.), *The Correspondence of Emily, Duchess of Leinster, 1731-1814*, 3 vols (Dublin, 1957) III, 141.

23 Sweeney, *The Sweeney Guide*, 39.

24 *ibid.*, 179.

25 FitzGerald, *Lady Louisa Conolly*, 107, 119.

26 NLI, Conolly Papers, MS 41,341/5, letter from J. Coghill, 18th October 1778.

27 Sweeney, *The Sweeney Guide*, 39.

28 TCD, Conolly Papers, MS 3955, MS 3939.

29. D'Arcy, *Horses, Lords and Racing Men*, 14.

30 *ibid.*, 15.

31 Ronan Lynch, *The Kirwans of Castlehacket, Co. Galway: history, folklore and mythology in an Irish horseracing family* (Dublin, 2006) 55.

32 Quoted in P. Livingstone, *The Fermanagh Story* (Enniskillen, 1969) 121.

33 Constantia Maxwell, *Country and Town in Ireland under the Georges* (London 1940; 1949 edn.) 34.

34 NA, Meath Papers, K/1/2 1827-33, 2210.

35 Quoted in Maxwell, *Country and Town in Ireland*, 33.

36 Quoted in Valerie Pakenham, *The Big House in Ireland* (London, n.d.) 129-30.

37 NLI, Doneraile Papers, MS 34,143(1), Hunting Journal of Hayes St Leger, 4th Viscount Doneraile, October 1837 – March 1838.

38 *ibid*. Information taken from the abstract to the papers.

39 D. Bourke, Earl of Mayo, and W.B. Boulton, *History of the Kildare Hunt* (London, 1913) 11.

40 Toby Barnard, Making the Grand Figure; lives and possessions in Ireland, 1641-1770 (Yale, 2004) 238.

41 Bourke and Boulton, *History of the Kildare Hunt*, 11.

42 TCD, Conolly Papers, MS 476, letter from Thos Thoroton, 7th June 1777.

43 *ibid*., MS 489, from same, 22 June 1777.

44 *ibid*., MS 496, letter from Lord Clifden, Gowran, 17th July 1777.

45 *ibid*., MS 381, Account of Conolly's estate since his coming of age, 4th March 1773.

46 IAA, Conolly Papers, J/9, 97/84, Castletown Accounts Day Book 1784-90; do. 1781-87, F104, 1787; F422, 'Work done at Dog Kennels Nov 1784 to May 1785'.

47 Patricia McCarthy, 'Buildings for Animals', *Art and Architecture of Ireland, Volume IV: Architecture 1600-2000* (Royal Irish Academy, Dublin, 2015) 380.

48 TCD, Conolly Papers, MS 3939, Tradesmen's Receipt Books 1778, v.1.

49 *ibid*., MSS 3974-84, letter from Chas. Kennedy, Johnstown, 4th July 1780, 'has imported fox cubs from Co. Waterford' for Tom Conolly.

50 FitzGerald, *Lady Louisa Conolly*, 151.

51 Lynch, *The Kirwans of Castlehacket*, 45.

52 IAA, Bunbury Letters, 94/84, from Lady Louisa Conolly to Tom Conolly, 12th April 1772 or 1773.

53 FitzGerald, *Lady Louisa Conolly*, 151.

54 Lena Boylan, 'Lady Louisa Conolly's Chip Hat Factory', *JKAS*, xv, 1971-76, 468-71.

55 McCarthy, 'Stables and Horses in Ireland', 28-71.

56 See 'The Devil and Tom Conolly: an eighteenth-century legend of Castletown by "A Broth of a Boy" (Russell)', first published in Dublin University Magazine, XXII, 1843, 677. A small section is reproduced in McCarthy, 'Stables and Horses in Ireland', 48.

57 FitzGerald, *Lady Louisa Conolly*, 44. This may have been called the 'Huntsmans Room' mentioned in accounts in 1762 in the Castletown Account Book 1762-64, IAA, Conolly Papers, 97/84.

58 NLI, Conolly MSS 5/4 1778, letter from Sir Wm Howe to Tom Conolly, 25th October 1778.

59 *ibid*., same to same, 12th July 1778.

60 Sweeney, *The Sweeney Guide*, 179.

61 A.P.W.Malcomson, 'The fall of the house of Conolly 1758-1803' in Allan Blackstock and Eoin Magennis (eds), *Politics and Political Culture in Britain and Ireland, 1750-1850: essays in tribute to Peter Jupp* (Belfast, 2007) 107-56.

62 *ibid*.

63 David Griffin, 'Castletown, Co. Kildare: the contribution of James, first Duke of Leinster', *Irish Architectural & Decorative Studies*, I, 1998, 120-45.

64 Ann Margaret Keller, 'The Long Gallery of Castletown House', *Bulletin of the Irish Georgian Society*, XXII, 1979, 1-54.

65 Lena Boylan, 'The Conollys of Castletown House', *Quarterly Bulletin of the Irish Georgian Society*, XI, no. 4, Oct-Dec 1968, 1-46.

66 D'Arcy, *Horses, Lords and Racing Men*, 27.

———

The wider Castletown: the designed landscape of the Wonderful Barn and Barn Hall

CÓILÍN Ó DRISCEOIL

THE MID-EIGHTEENTH-CENTURY GRANARY KNOWN AS THE WONDERFUL BARN (PLATE 1), 1.8km north-east of Castletown House, has been well researched by scholars and is widely celebrated for its idiosyncratic 'corkscrew' architecture.[1] By way of contrast, the designed landscape that surrounds the Wonderful Barn and Barn Hall has been largely overlooked. This is undeserved, for the Wonderful Barn forms just one element in this farm complex (Plate 2), which is in many ways as innovative and modernising as the barn itself. This paper draws on archaeological excavations to recreate the mid-eighteenth-century layout of Barn Hall, its farm buildings and walled garden, and also highlights the probable role of the gentleman farmer Joseph Cooper.

When the Wonderful Barn was constructed in 1743, the Barn Hall estate, comprising sixty-one hectares in the townlands of Barnhall and Rinawade Upper and Lower, was leased by the Conollys to Joseph Cooper (d.1786) (Plate 3).[2] A stone plaque above the main west entrance to the Wonderful Barn bears an inscription '1743 execut'd by John Glinn' (Plate 6). The 1740 Conolly rent rolls record that a John Glinn was resident at Pound Street in Leixlip, on the site of the current Glebe House.[3] In 1786 the travel writer William Wilson wrote that Glinn had built the Wonderful Barn for the Conolly family.[4] The Wonderful Barn does not appear on the two eighteenth-century estate maps commissioned by the Conolly family, nor on John Rocque's 1760 map of the county of Dublin that did depict Castletown and other surrounding demesnes. Many of the eighteenth-century documents suggest that the prospect of the Wonderful Barn from Castletown House was not particularly significant, although its appearance in the 1752 Nobel and Keenan map, the 1783 James Taylor map and the 1744 Baylie and Mooney map of Carton demesne suggest otherwise.[5] The tree-lined avenue linking the barn and

1 – Archaeological excavation of one of the small dovecotes in the north-east courtyard next to the wonderful Barn (all photos by the author unless otherwise stated)

2– *Barn Hall and the Wonderful Barn, from west, 1968 (courtesy Irish Architectural Archive)*

3– *Map of Joseph Cooper's Barn Hall estate (based on the 1837 Ordnance Survey map)*

4 – *First edition Ordnance Survey map of Barn Hall, 1837 (courtesy Ordnance Survey of Ireland)*

opposite 5 – *Barn Hall, layout and summary archaeological excavation plan*

Building descriptions in square parenthesis are taken from the Griffith's Valuation House Books

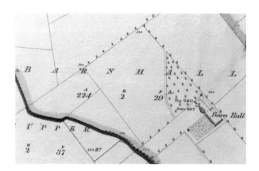

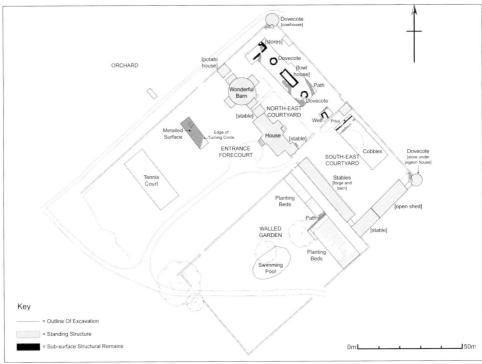

*6 – Plaque over front entrance commemorating the builder John Glinn's work
on the Wonderful Barn in 1743*

the house today was laid out in the mid-nineteenth century and enjoyed from the first-floor
windows on the east side (now the Blue Bedroom).

In 1759 Thomas Conolly drew up (or renewed?) a lease to Joseph Cooper, 'farmer',
for the 'Houses, Outhouses, Barns, Buildings, Gardens, Orchards' at Barn Hall.[6] Joseph
Cooper came from a family of agricultural improvers and landscape designers. His residence at Barn Hall suggests that he may have been involved in the design of the
Wonderful Barn and/or its courtyards and walled gardens. Today much of Barn Hall survives relatively intact – despite spates of vandalism – as a detached two-storey, seven-
bay house sited immediately beside the Wonderful Barn. Behind the house and barn
stand two walled courtyards, and a walled garden lies to the south-west (Plates 2, 5).
Most of the original entrance court survives, as does an open area north of the barn that
may have been an orchard. Whilst the general topography of Joseph Cooper's courtyard
farm at Barn Hall can be reconstructed from these standing remains and the nineteenth-
century Ordnance Survey (OS) maps, written records that might reveal the functions of
the two courtyards and the various buildings they contain are lacking (Plate 4). Similarly,
historical information is wanting on the layout of the eighteenth-century walled garden
and its planting arrangements, and on the make-up of the entrance court area. To address
these gaps, archaeological research excavations and geophysical surveys were under-

7 – Excavations underway at the entrance forecourt Barn Hall
(taken from west)

taken at Barn Hall in 2015-16. What follows is a summary of the key outcomes of the investigations.[7]

Excavations immediately to the west of the main entrance into the Wonderful Barn revealed a metalled surface of spreads of hard, highly compacted gravel and small angular stones. This was defined on the south by a rough kerb of larger rounded stones, probably part of a turning circle for carts and coaches (Plates 5, 7). Repairs to potholes in the metalled surface were evident in the form of tightly packed settings of rounded large stones and crushed red-brick. The hard surfacing and turning circle documented in the excavation formed part of an impressive prospect that was created by the front (west) façade of Barn Hall and the Wonderful Barn. The visual impact of this façade was maximised by deliberately obstructing views towards the house until visitors had turned the north-west corner of the walled garden and had moved into the main avenue forecourt (Plate 13).

The excavations in the north-east courtyard revealed the foundations of two curious 3.75m-diameter freestanding circular structures (Plates 1, 7). A horse skull was buried beneath the clay floor of the northernmost example, perhaps as a good-luck token. The circular structures are marked on the historic OS maps but without a function being ascribed to them (Plate 4). However, a compelling analogy is to be found at Whitehall,

*8 – Dovecote (built c. 1742) of similar form to those at Barn Hall,
at the White Barn, Whitehall, Co Dublin*

county Dublin, where a freestanding conical dovecote of similar dimensions (3.5m external diameter) stands intact next to the White Barn, built in 1742 by Major Hall, who was,
like Joseph Cooper, a lessee of the Castletown estate (Plate 8).[8] The extant dovecotes
built at the corners of the courtyards at Barn Hall are also somewhat similar, though much
larger. Other direct parallels from Ireland are unknown, but an English example is
recorded at Harlyn House, Cornwall.[9]

The dovecotes were positioned on either side of a 9.3m x 3.8m rectangular structure which can be equated with a 'fowl house' mentioned in the Griffith's Valuation
House Books (Plates 5, 9).[10] At the north end of the north-east courtyard, a 8.7m x 4.15m
rectangular building, termed a 'store' in the House Books, was also uncovered, and at
the opposite side of the yard a blocked rectangular stone well was excavated. Further dis-
coveries included a diagonal cobbled path that led from the rear (east) entrance of the
Wonderful Barn towards the standing conical dovecote in the north-east corner of the
yard, and further diagonal paths of gravel on the south side of the yard. Surfacing elsewhere comprised pounded stones, which were probably originally covered over with a
thin layer of gravel and clay. This form of metalling together with the direct link between
the yard and the barn suggest that the north-east courtyard was primarily a stack-yard,
where dried corn was brought for stacking before being threshed. But while the court-

*9 – Excavation area in the north-east courtyard, showing (left to right) foundations of rectangular
store building, diagonal cobbled pathway, a dovecote on either side of a 'fowl house'*

yard was primarily a utilitarian space for processing grain for storage in the granary, the
ornamental dovecotes, probably better considered as ornamental follies rather than sub-
stantively functional broiler houses, provided a polite, formal and somewhat idiosyncratic element to this space.[11]

The excavations uncovered a finely cobbled yard surface with channels and a distinctive north-south camber to facilitate drainage in the south-east courtyard, below later
clay make-up deposits (Plate 5). Three pedestals sat proud of the cobbles and were possibly the remains of hitching posts for horses. Part of the south wall and the internal dividing wall between the two privies documented in the House Books and marked on the
nineteenth-century OS maps were also revealed in the north of the courtyard, alongside
a cobbled path. The House Books provide some indication of how these buildings were
used (Plate 5). Corn-producing farms such as Barn Hall required many horses for plough-
ing and a myriad of other tasks, and large stables were required. These were located on
the west side of the south range, beside an open-sided hay shed, used presumably to store
hay for fodder and straw for bedding. A forge to supply the farmstead with iron tools and
to shoe horses was located in the west range, beside another barn, which was probably
used to store feed for the animals. The farm buildings, along with the cobbling and
drainage, suggest that the south-east courtyard was a solely utilitarian space that serv-

iced the estate farm, an interpretation underlined by the absence of any direct access to the more polite space of the north-east courtyard.

THE WALLED GARDEN

THE EXCAVATIONS IN THE ONE-ACRE WALLED GARDEN UNCOVERED A CENTRAL 2.5M-wide path surfaced with crushed lime-mortar and running north-east to south-west (Plates 5, 10). Two well-defined planting-holes, probably for ornamental trees, were noted on the north side of the path and there were some indications of border planting alongside it. Accordingly, the walled garden was laid out to a fairly standard plan, being divided into four equal blocks by cross-paths. The paths would have been lined with a narrow border which was planted with flowers; daisy was identified in the archaeobotanical assessment.[12] Interesting information on planting techniques in the walled garden was also brought to light by the excavations. Five distinct planting plots were recorded within the excavated area, two in the quadrant to the south of the path and four in that to the north (Plate 11). All of the planting features had been cut into an introduced subsoil horizon that contained coins of George I (1719-24) and George II (1737-

10 – Excavations underway in the walled garden of Barn Hall (from north)

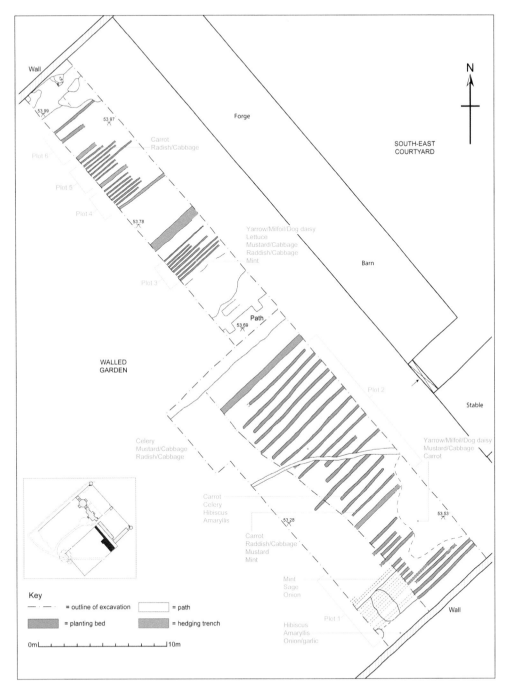

11 – Excavated planting beds and paths in the Barn Hall walled garden.
Botanical remains from soil samples are noted in green.

(all drawings by Philip Kenny, Kilkenny Archaeology)

38), thereby dating the construction of the walled garden to around the time of Joseph Cooper's tenure at Barn Hall. There was no indication that the excavated planting features overlay an earlier gardening layout, and their geometry also differed markedly from the diagonal paths that are shown on the first edition OS map (Plate 4). Accordingly, the planting layout revealed by the walled garden's excavation is most probably the primary, mid-eighteenth-century gardening layout. The planting plots contained rows of narrow 20cm-wide x 3-8cm-deep linear trenches that ran parallel to the central path and were spaced on average 20-30cm apart, with the exception of those in the plot immediately south of the path, which were spaced at 50cm intervals. The plots were defined into distinctive groups by 40cm wide hedging trenches (Plate 11). The spacing of the planting rows accords well with Duff's recommendations from 1807 that cabbage drills should be two feet apart and herbs and Brussels sprouts should be two to two-and-a-half feet apart.[13] Drills six inches apart may have been used for nursery planting or for salad crops. The arrangement of long narrow drills, and to a certain extent the plants identified in the archaeobotanical analysis (see below), indicate that the walled garden was effectively a Georgian kitchen garden or 'potager' – a productive garden whose primary purpose was to keep the kitchen supplied with fresh vegetables and fruit.

The soils in the planting rows were enhanced with manure that contained molluscs, which raises the pH of acidic soils, and ash and charcoal, which is also added to improve soil quality. Archaeobotanical analysis of soil samples from the rows suggested the charcoal derived from pruning offcuts, which was probably burnt as part of garden waste and incorporated with other organic material (for example, dung and household waste) into the soils as a fertilizer. Beranger's 1766 view of Monkstown castle appears to show gardeners digging closely spaced linear drills of similar form to those recorded at Barn Hall, and other good comparisons for the Wonderful Barn planting trenches have been noted in excavations at Castle Bromwich, Birmingham and Aberglasney Gardens, Carmarthenshire (Plate 12). Excavations at both gardens produced planting beds that were also heavily manured and comparable in size and spacing intervals to those at Barn Hall.[14] The trenches on both sites were interpreted as bedding trenches for plants, although an alternative suggestion that they were 'dug to hold manure below a deeper, rectangular planting bed' was made.[15]

Seeds and charcoal recovered from the archaeobotanical analysis of soil samples allow for some insights into the plant species that were growing in and around Barn Hall's walled garden in the eighteenth century (Plate 11).[16] Seeds from the mint/deadnettle, mustard/cabbage, mallow and carrot families were identified, and some were probably grown in smaller vegetable or herb gardens within the larger enclosure of the walled garden. Charcoals from willow/poplar, cherry-type, walnut, holly, pomaceous fruitwoods and beech were also found, representing a mix of fruit and nut trees along with species suitable for hedging and borders. Such tree species were commonly recorded on large Irish late seventeenth-century estates. Some assumptions can also be made regarding other planting in the walled garden. The longest walls were orientated east-west to maximise

12 – 'Monckstown' by Gabriel Beranger (1766)

*The painting of Monkstown Castle, Co Dublin, appears to show gardeners digging drills of similar form to those
excavated in the walled garden at Barn Hall (courtesy National Library of Ireland)*

the space available to train fruits such as apricots, peaches and nectarines along the warmest north wall.[17] The east and west walls would typically have been used for growing hardier fruits such as cherry, apples, pears and plums, whilst the coolest south wall was used for hardier species like filberts and Morello cherries (Plate 13). A glasshouse may also have been used, and some of the broken glass retrieved in the excavation may have originated from such a structure.

The creation of Barn Hall in the 1740s coincided with the movement to modernise the rural economy which saw a cohort of 'improving landlords' implementing the latest scientific developments in tillage farming, animal husbandry, land reclamation and land enclosure in order to increase output. The physical landscape created at Barn Hall bears all the hallmarks of the type of landed estate where the 'New Farming' promoted by the likes of Stephen Switzer, Jethro Tull and Robert Molesworth would have been practiced.[18] Furthermore, the topography and the 'formal ordering of plan and façade' that is seen at Barn Hall connects it to a small number of other Irish early Georgian 'courtyard farms'.[19] Barn Hall, together with the Wonderful Barn, is an instance of innovation and progress in the wider Castletown landscape.

———

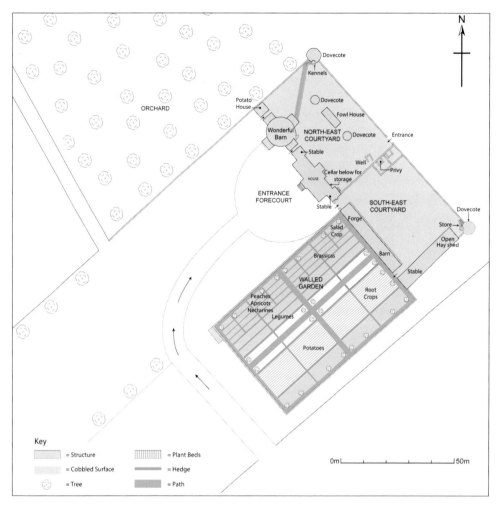

13 – Reconstruction plan of Joseph Cooper's Barn Hall, c.1770,
showing the entrance route which was designed to give maximum visual effect to the impressive
facade formed by the Wonderful Barn and Barn Hall

ACKNOWLEDGEMENTS

Funding for the archaeological project at Barn Hall was provided by the Parks Department, Kildare County Council, and the assistance of Fergal O'Donovan of that department is gratefully acknowledged. I wish to acknowledge the work of the excavation and post-excavation team: Philip Kenny, Barry Fitzgibbon, Béa Ní Dhrisceoil, Philip Kavanagh, Padraig Crawford, Cara O'Doherty, Susan Lyons, Dan Lenehan and Earthsound Geophysics. Dr Finola O'Kane Crimmins also assisted with documentary material relating to the Castletown estate, and kindly answered various queries. Finally, thanks to John Colgan for sharing his insights into the history of Barn Hall and the Castletown estate.

ENDNOTES

1 Lord Walter Fitzgearld, 'Castletown and its owners', *Journal of the Kildare Archaeological Society,* vol. 2, no. 6, 1898, 377; Lena Boylan, 'The Wonderful Barn', *Journal of the County Kildare Archaeological Society*, 28, pt. 3, 1997, 337-47; James Howley, *The Follies and Garden Buildings of Ireland* (Yale, 2004) 211-15; John Colgan, *Leixlip, County Kildare* (Leixlip, 2005) 231; Finola O'Kane Crimmins, 'The Wonderful Barn, Historic Landscape Assessment Report', unpublished report for Kildare County Council, 2011.

2 Boylan, 'Wonderful Barn', 343. In 1773 a further seventy acres at Parsonstown was leased to the estate.

3 Colgan, *Leixlip*, 231.

4 William Wilson, *The Post-Chaise Companion or Traveller's Directory Through Ireland* (Dublin, 1786) 99; Fitzgearld, 'Castletown and its owners', 377; Boylan, 'Wonderful Barn', 339; Colgan, *Leixlip*, 231; Howley, *Follies and Garden Buildings*, 212, 214.

5 O'Kane Crimmins, 'Wonderful Barn', 11.

6 Boylan, 'Wonderful Barn', 343-44.

7 Cóilín Ó Drisceoil and Barry Fitzgibbon, 'Archaeological Excavations 2015-16 at the Wonderful Barn, Leixlip, Co Kildare, 15E0324, Final Report' (Kilkenny Archaeology, 2017).

8 Howley, *Follies and Garden Buildings*, 211-12.

9 https://historicengland.org.uk/listing/the-list/list-entry/1212749 (accessed 7th March 2018).

10 The Griffith's Valuation 'House Books' contain descriptions of the farm buildings that surrounded the house and barn in 1842 and 1850, and by comparing the measurements given in the House Books to the excavated buildings and those marked on the 1837 Ordnance Survey map, it is possible to assign functions to many of these structures. The House Books for Barn Hall are available from the National Archives of Ireland online at: http://census.nationalarchives.ie/search/vob/house_books.jsp (accessed 7th March 2018).

11 Peter Hansell and Jean Hansell, *Dovecotes* (Oxford, 2010) 26-38.

12 Ó Drisceoil and Fitzgibbon, 'Excavations at the Wonderful Barn', 82-89.

13 George Duff, *The Vegetable Garden, Containing the Names and Qualities of the most approved vegetables* (Dublin, 1842) 37.

14 Chris K. Currie and Martin Locock, 'Excavations at Castle Bromwich Hall gardens 1981-91', *Post-medieval Archaeology*, 27, 1993, 124; Kevin Blockley and Ian Halfpenney, *Aberglasney House and Gardens: archaeology, history and architecture*, British Archaeological Reports, British Series, 334 (Oxford, 2005) 73-74. Chris K. Currie, *Garden Archaeology, A Handbook*, Council for British Archaeology Practical Handbook, no. 17 (York, 2005) fig. 26.

15 Blockley and Halfpenney, *Aberglasney House and Gardens*, 74.

16 Ó Drisceoil and Fitzgibbon, 'Excavations at the Wonderful Barn', 82-89.

17 John Watkins and Tom Wright (eds), *The Management and Maintenance of Historic Parks, Gardens and Landscapes*, English Heritage Handbook (London, 2007) 204.

18 John Feehan, *Farming in Ireland: history, heritage and environment* (Dublin, 2003) 93-96.

19 Frederick H.A. Aalen, Kevin Whelan and Matthew Stout (eds), *Atlas of the Irish Rural Landscape* (2nd edn., Cork, 2011) 226-27.

———

The history of the Castletown collections, 1720-1960

AIDAN O'BOYLE

THE LONG GALLERY AT CASTLETOWN WAS ORIGINALLY DESIGNED AS A PICTURE gallery, but owing to the death of William 'Speaker' Conolly in 1729 the room was left unfinished.[1] It is unclear whether Speaker Conolly had already formed the nucleus of a collection or whether his nephew, William James Conolly (d.1754), laid the foundations of the family collection at Castletown. William James was the first member of the family to make the Grand Tour, in 1726-27. His marriage to Lady Anne Wentworth in 1733 brought many works of art into the Conolly collection, although many of these remained in England and, as discussed elsewhere in this volume, never made it to Castletown. The purpose of this article is to give a general overview of the Conolly collection's formation, focusing on the two most important phases of its development, *c*.1760-1800 and *c*.1850-76. The three key figures are Tom Conolly (1738-1803), his wife Lady Louisa Lennox (1743-1821), and the less well-known Thomas Conolly MP (1823-1876), who inherited Castletown in 1858. Ebullient, extravagant and not particularly cultured, he completed a grand tour in 1870-71 and made one or two important contributions to the family collection.[2] No eighteenth- or early nineteenth-century inventories of Castletown's contents are known to exist, and the earliest surviving inventory of Castletown House was compiled in 1893-94. On its own it would be of little use were it not for a surviving contemporary photographic record of the interior.[3] Other photographs reproduced in Vol. V of the *Georgian Society Records* in 1913, and later photographs and sales catalogues from the 1960s, also help to build up as rounded a picture as possible of the original collection and the connected hanging and arrangement of the Green Drawing Room and the dining room, two key ground-floor rooms.

When Castletown's ground-floor rooms were being remodelled in the 1760s, Tom and Louisa Conolly moved to Leixlip Castle. Lady Louisa's correspondence for the years 1764-68 contains general references to the building work rather than to any one room in

1 – Pompeo Girolamo Batoni (1708-1778), JOHN STAPLES (1734-1820) OF LYSSAN, CO TYRONE
1773, oil on canvas, 249 x 175 cm (Museo di Roma)

particular, with the exception of the new dining room. A small number of payments for textiles used in the ground-floor rooms are recorded in her accounts for the period 1767-75. She purchased three small paintings from the Dublin branch of Josiah Wedgwood's shop on 2nd April 1775, though it is unclear what genre they were.[4] Payments for pictures are also found in Tom Conolly's accounts of 1767-70. Of particular interest are the four payments (ranging in price from £10 to £68 5s) to the artist Robert Healy between 2nd November 1767 and 30th January 1770 that relate to the important series of equestrian pictures that was once at Castletown. He also made a payment of £34 2s 6d on 31st October 1769 to his brother-in-law, John Staples, for several paintings Staples had bought on Lady Louisa's behalf.[5] An undated letter from Lady Sarah Lennox to her sister Emily, Duchess of Leinster described a similar commission to buy paintings on the Conollys' behalf:

> Dear Sister,
>
> I told you a story about Smiths pictures in saying they were rather dear, for I have seen them myself & must give you an account of them.
>
> There are large finished pictures of 60, 40, 30 & 20 pound. [There] are small finished ones of 16, 14, 10, pound, there are largish unfinished ones, of 5, 4, 3, guineas, &...
>
> Now the unfinished are thus, one clump in the foreground is quite finished, the background wants the finishing touches, or else the whole is the dead colouring & a second touch, but not the last high finish which Smith was so famous for. Where there [are] no figures of cattle the unfinished look like common paint[ed] finished landscapes. Many look as if they might be highly finished by a little finishing to a hill or a distant clump, & in short all are prettily colour'd & designed, all the skies are finished as to colouring [though] not blended together.
>
> I have bought 5 for 5.5 [guineas] that in my mind are beautiful & were thought so by Mrs Smith who is a very good judge. Ly Louisa has also bought some. I am so certain that my sister Louisa will like them that I shall venture to lay out ten guineas for her in 2 or 3 of the small, (almost as finished) sort, for I am sure she will never forgive me losing an [opportunity] which can never be regained of buying such pretty things so cheap ... I don't know your taste ... I therefore beg you will write me your order directly & your directions for what you like best, figures, cattle, castles, cottages ... water, [or] snow pieces...[6]

This letter, dated *c*.1776/77, provides a revealing insight into the sisters' attitudes to paintings and their acquisition. Bargain-hunting rather than connoisseurship was to the fore, with the works of the English landscape artist William Smith of Chichester (1707-1764) very much to their taste. The role of clumps of trees in contemporary landscape design was evidently much appreciated. Individual paintings appear to have been acquired less for their aesthetic value than for their decorative potential. In the absence of any eighteenth-century pictorial evidence, the Castletown print room of 1768 reveals much about

Lady Louisa's personal choice in paintings, her taste in picture frames and the decorative manner in which she would have hung her closets and dressing rooms. The print room suggests that she arranged her paintings with a symmetrical formality, selecting the most elaborate frames for paintings of the greatest personal interest. There was a short-lived fashion in the 1760s for hanging paintings with elaborate decorative cords with bows and tassels. How widespread this method of display was is unclear, but it was used by George III and Queen Charlotte at Buckingham House in 1763 and by Lady Louisa Conolly at Castletown in the late 1760s.[7] Such hanging methods were by their very nature ephemeral, and the only surviving indication of Lady Louisa's preference lies in the fictive gilt cords, bows and tassels of Richard Cranfield's pier glasses in the dining room at Castletown.

Although Tom Conolly was painted by Anton Raphael Mengs during his grand tour, this does not necessarily indicate a substantial interest in the arts. The only note-worthy Irish artists that he patronised were George Barrett and Robert Healy, with the former documenting his estate and the latter his sporting interests. In 1784 he commissioned four landscapes of Castletown from the London-based Irish artist Edmund Garvey (1740-1813), discussed elsewhere in this volume (see pp.156-60).[8] He also patronised another London-based Irish artist, the miniaturist Richard Bull (active 1777-1809). Bull discussed his portrait of Tom Conolly in a letter to William Robert, 2nd Duke of Leinster:

> May it please your Grace,
>
> When Mr Conolly was here last he did me the honour of sitting for his picture, which he was so kind to promise to show your Grace, as I was ambitious that your Grace might see what improvement I have made. Mr Conolly having expressed a wish to have it engraved which I suppose had his time permitted would have been executed. By Mr Conolly's permission I have taken an exact copy of it only higher finished, having more time to complete it. It is in the hands of the first engraver here & if anything can stamp an additional value on a print of such illustrious character, it must be dedicating it to your grace. I would not presume to take such a liberty without your Graces Approbation. The Engraver has promised to have it finished in six weeks. If your grace approves & will The Engraver has promised to have it finished in six weeks. If your grace approves & will favour me with the number you wish to have for your friends I shall take care to have the very best impressions carefully delivered. There will be a few proofs touched, colour'd & plain, although executed in the first manner the price of the prints will be moderate 3/6 plain, colour'd 7/6...
>
> I remain with the highest respect your graces most Dutiful & very humble Servt.
>
> Richard Bull.[9]

Bull, who was educated at the Dublin Society Schools, moved to London c.1790, where he worked successfully for a large and fashionable clientele. While in London in 1795, Tom Conolly had commissioned Bull to paint his portrait and to have it engraved, with the artist hoping to dedicate the engraving to the Duke of Leinster.[10]

The Green Drawing Room, or Saloon, given its central position and status, was the most important of the ground-floor State Rooms. It was remodelled and redecorated during the period 1764-68, when Tom Conolly's accounts record a substantial payment of two £223 1s 5d to Richard Cranfield on 28th September 1768 for carving and gilding work to the drawing rooms and dining room in a manner similar to the State Rooms at Leinster House, upon which they were based. By the 1760s the Saloon and Red Drawing Room had been hung with the expensive fabrics that were considered the most appropriate backdrop for displaying paintings and replacing Castletown's original panelled interiors of the 1720s.[11]

The earliest records of the picture-hang in the Green Drawing Room date from the late nineteenth century. They describe the dense, saturated Italianate method of picture-hanging common to the *salone* of the great palazzi of Florence and Rome and experienced by grand tourists such as Tom Conolly. Many eighteenth-century great houses were laid out with visitors in mind, with rooms of parade intended for entertaining on a grand scale. Works were frequently hung not by style, genre or subject matter, but by size and frame-type. The quality of individual paintings varied considerably, and works of secondary importance, or copies, were also frequently included. The rationale for this approach was to impress the viewer with the scale, density and richness of the room's overall ensemble, of which the paintings formed an essential part. The frames were fixed to the walls using a variety of methods, including the bows and tassels favoured by Lady Louisa, and the frames' design was often repeated in the gilt, walnut or ebonised furniture arranged symmetrically beneath them.

In the early nineteenth century, the Prince Regent, a great connoisseur of seventeenth-century Dutch painting, sometimes confined himself to single-file picture-hangs in rooms such as the Blue Velvet Room at Carlton House.[12] Surviving nineteenth-century photographs of Castletown reveal that Thomas Conolly chose a single-file picture-hang as part of the *c*.1870 redecoration of the Red Drawing Room (see p.112). The earliest surviving Castletown inventory, dating from 1893-94 provides a wealth of useful information on the Victorian single-file picture-hang, which consisted almost exclusively of religious paintings and amounted to eighteen pictures in total. By cross-referencing this inventory with late nineteenth-century and early twentieth-century photographs, it is possible to identify some of the works, most of which were copies after Old Master paintings.[13] Above the door leading into the Green Drawing Room hung a copy of Raphael's *Madonna della Seggiola*. In the centre of the east wall hung a reduced copy of Veronese's *Feast at the House of Simon*, previously in the collection of the Earl of Shaftesbury. The largest painting in the room was a full-scale copy of *The Virgin and Child with Saints Jerome, Mary Magdalene and Angels* by Correggio (1489-1534), which hung on the east wall in the late nineteenth century before being re-hung over the chimney piece *c*.1912 (Plate 2). This copy by Giovanni Mazzolini (d.1876) was acquired in Rome in 1871 by Thomas Conolly. Mazzolini was a well-known copyist working in Rome in the mid- to late-nineteenth century, and it is possible that he may have also provided Conolly with several other copies which hung in the Red Drawing Room.

Thomas Conolly showed little evidence of connoisseurship in hanging his newly redecorated drawing room with a series of copies after well-known Italian Renaissance paintings. There was, however, one important exception to the rule – a rare work of impeccable provenance by the seventeenth-century Spanish master Bartolomé Esteban Murillo (1617-1682), which hung just to the left of the chimney piece. Spanish works, which had been rare in Irish collections prior to the Napoleonic Wars, were now much sought-after by collectors. The painting in question, *Christ after the Flagellation*, is now in the collection of the Krannert Art Museum at the University of Illinois (Plate 3). It is one of only two versions of the subject painted by the artist. The painting was in the collection of King Louis-Philippe of France, who installed it in his famous 'Spanish Gallery' at the Louvre in 1842, from whence it was removed following the Revolution of 1848. King Louis-Philippe's collection was sold following his death in England in 1850.[14] It is likely that Conolly acquired the painting in London at the auction of the late king's collection at Christie's in May 1853, for later that year he lent it to the Irish Industrial Art Exhibition in Dublin. The work, which was listed in the exhibition catalogue as No. 48, *The Saviour*

2 – The Red Drawing Room, looking south-east in 1912
(from The Georgian Society Records, V, 1913, pl.XXVIII)

3 – Bartolome Esteban Murillo, CHRIST AFTER THE FLAGELLATION
c.1670, oil on canvas, 127 x 146 cm (Krannert Art Museum, University of Illinois)

opposite 4 – The dining room at Castletown in 1912
(from THE GEORGIAN SOCIETY RECORDS, V, 1912, pl.XXVII)

being Scourged, was without doubt the most important painting acquired by the Conolly family in the nineteenth-century.[15]

The dining room at Castletown was created by Tom and Lady Louisa Conolly in the 1760s and contained a considerable number of family paintings, totalling twenty-three in number by the end of the nineteenth century. With the exception of one or two genre paintings, and an enlarged copy of Raphael's *School of Athens*, the majority of the paintings were portraits.[16] Little had changed by the time the room was photographed by the Irish Georgian Society in 1912 (Plate 4). Charles Jervas' matching portraits of Speaker Conolly and his wife Katherine, being of the right size and shape, served as overdoors, and they were balanced on the opposite wall by another pair in identical frames. The matching size of the paintings and the uniformity of the eighteenth-century picture frames would suggest that they had been placed there as part of the original decorative scheme in the 1760s.Though they are no longer in their original position, all but one of the four paintings is still at Castletown. Above the chimney piece hung a magnificent full-length portrait in a gilded neoclassical frame surmounted by an urn. This work, the focal point of the room, was a portrait of John Staples (1734-1820) of Lyssan, county Tyrone, by

Pompeo Batoni. Staples was the husband of Lady Harriet Conolly, sister of Tom Conolly, whom he had married in 1764. Due to his brother-in-law's influence, Staples was elected to the Irish House of Commons as MP for Newtown Limavady in 1765. Following the early death of his wife, he departed for Italy, visiting Florence, Capua, Naples, Rome and Venice between 1772 and 1774.

While Tom Conolly had patronised Mengs, Staples preferred his more fashionable rival Batoni, then at the height of his powers. The sitter is depicted full-length against an idealised classical landscape, his hand resting on the pedestal of the Ludovisi Mars, a work praised by Winckelmann[17] and frequently used by Batoni as a prop in his paintings (Plate 1). Other props which recur in Batoni's paintings are the Corinthian capital and the fragment of broken frieze surmounted by a griffin which appeared in over a dozen paintings. This work, which is regarded as an exemplary of its genre, is signed and dated 'P. BATONI PINXIT ROMAE / ANNO 1773'. No evidence has so far come to light which would indicate how or under what circumstances the painting arrived at Castletown. Tom Conolly and John Staples must have been close, with Staples certainly owing his political career to Conolly, and it is possible that it was given to his brother-in-law in gratitude or in friendship. The painting and its neoclassical frame were an almost exact fit for the space above the chimney piece and it may therefore have formed part of the original picture-hang of the room.

Two notable pieces of sculpture also formed part of the Castletown collection. The

first was a janiform herm of Brutus and Seneca joined in the Antique Manner after the two-faced god, Janus. This uncommon work by an unidentified eighteenth-century sculptor was most likely produced in Italy for the Grand Tour market. Though there is no documentary evidence to support it, it is probable that this double-headed herm, representing Brutus and Seneca as *Man of Thought and Man of Action*, had been acquired by Tom Conolly on his grand tour in 1758. Busts of Brutus and Seneca were popular with eighteenth-century collectors, and were widely copied. The Antique model for the frowning Brutus is now believed to represent the Athenian orator Demosthenes. The bust can be seen in a photograph of the entrance hall taken in the late nineteenth century.[18] The second sculpture is a copy of *A Boy with a Dolphin* after Bartolomeo Cavaceppi (1716-1799). The original was first advertised by Cavaceppi in 1768 as a work by Raphael executed by Lorenzetti.[19] The work was popular, and versions exist in the State Hermitage Museum in St Petersburg, at Tsarskoe Selo, at Ickworth, at Althorp, and in various other collections. It was copied by, among others, Joseph Nollekens (1737-1823), in whose workshop the Castletown version was produced.[20] Given that Nollekens did not arrive in Rome until 1761, the work could not have been acquired by Tom Connolly on his grand tour. It seems probable, therefore, that this sculpture belongs to the second phase of collecting at Castletown, and was most likely purchased by Thomas Conolly MP while in Rome *c.*1870.

Irish country house collections of the eighteenth and nineteenth centuries tended to contain a great many works of mixed quality; Castletown was no exception. For the most part, paintings were acquired for decorative purposes to furnish interiors rather than for their intrinsic merit as individual works of art. It is evident from both the archival and photographic records that the picture-hangs in Castletown's reception rooms were altered several times between Tom and Lady Louisa Conolly's redecoration in the 1760s and the family's sale of the contents in1966. With some notable exceptions to the rule, the documentary record shows little evidence of connoisseurship in successive generations of the Connolly family. Instead, a strong desire to record for posterity the portraits of family members and friends, their horses, and their estate emerges.

———

ACKNOWLEDGEMENTS

I wish to thank the staff of the Irish Architectural Archive for their assistance, in particular, Aisling Dunne and Anne Henderson. Likewise, I am grateful to the staff of the Manuscript Department at Trinity College Dublin, the National Library of Ireland and the Royal Irish Academy. I would also like to thank Dr Suzanne Pegley, David Griffin, Liam Brady and Mary Heffernan (OPW) for their assistance.

ENDNOTES

The following abbreviations are used:

IAA	Irish Architectural Archive
NLI	National Library of Ireland
TCD	Trinity College Dublin

1   Ann Keller, '"In Great Vogue'; the Long Gallery at Castletown', in Elizabeth Mayes (ed.), *Castletown, Decorative Arts* (OPW, Trim, 2011) 57.

2   Suzanne Pegley, 'Landscapes of Power: the social network of the power elite in mid-Victorian Ireland, case study of Thomas Conolly (1823-76) of Castletown, Co Kildare', unpublished PhD thesis, Maynooth University, 2017.

3   IAA, photographs in the Castletown box files.

4   TCD, Conolly Papers, MS 3966, Accounts of Lady Louisa Conolly.

5   *ibid.*, MS 3964, Accounts of Tom Conolly.

6   NLI, Leinster Papers, MS 619, Lady Sarah Lennox to Emily, Duchess of Leinster, regarding the purchase of paintings by William Smith of Chichester (1707-1764) for, and by Lady Louisa Conolly. *c.*1776-1777.

7   John Fowler and John Cornforth, *English Decoration in the Eighteenth Century* (Barrie & Jenkins, London, 1974) 233.

8   NLI, Thomas Conolly Papers, MS 4,341/9, Edmund Garvey, 7 Bow Street, London, to Thomas Conolly, 22nd May 1784.

9   NLI, Leinster Papers, MS 41,552/40, Richard Bull, Miniaturist, 101 Pall Mall, London, to William Robert, Duke of Leinster, 4 September 1795.

10   A copy of this engraving has been found in the collection of the National Gallery of Ireland (NGI 10,753, but the whereabouts of the original miniature is unknown.

11   John Cornforth, *Early Georgian Interiors* (Yale, 2004) 95. According to Cornforth, the fashion for hanging saloons and drawing rooms with fabric other than tapestry owed its origin to the rise in the number of art collections formed in the first half of the eighteenth century.

12   David Watkin, *The Royal Interiors of Regency England* (Vendome Press, New York, 1984) 122.

13   IAA, Castletown Papers, J/11, Inventory 1893-94 (amended in 1898) of Castletown.

14   Suzanne L. Stratton-Pruitt (ed.), *Bartolomé Esteban Murillo (1617-1682), Paintings from American Collections* (Harry Abrams, New York, 2002) 160-61.

15   *ibid.*

16   A.M. Stewart, *Irish Art Loan Exhibitions 1765-1927*, 3 vols (Manton, Dublin, 1990) II, 495.

17   IAA, Castletown Papers, J/11, Inventory 1893-94 (amended in 1898) of Castletown.

18   Various authors, *Citizens and Kings: portraits in the age of revolution, 1760-1830* (Royal Academy of Arts, London, 2007) 294, no. 61. Sotheby's, London, Old Master Sculpture and Works of Art, lot 109, 3rd December 2014, www.sothebys.com/en/auctions/ecatalogue/2014/ols-masterssculpture-works-art-l14233lot.109.hmtl.

19   Sotheby's, *ibid.*

20   Sotheby's, European Sculpture and Works of Art, 9th July, 2004, lot 101. www.sothebys.com /en/auctions/ecatalogue/2004/european-sculpture-works-of-art-9001900-104231/lot.101.hmtl.

———

The conservation of the Red Drawing Room at Castletown

CHRISTOPHER MOORE

T HIS PAPER ADDRESSES THE RESEARCH AND CONSERVATION PROCESS THAT HAS INFORMED recent conservation works in the Crimson or Red Drawing Room at Castletown. Known simply as the Red Drawing Room since 1967, the recent conservation works in this room have been a collaboration between the Office of Public Works (OPW) and the Castletown Foundation, with grant aid from the Apollo Foundation.[1] The underlying philosophy of the works has been to secure the decoration of the room as a totality. This includes both the grandeur of Tom and Lady Louisa Conolly's1760s creation as well as the decorative refiguring of the early 1870s. Despite the vicissitudes from which the house suffered in the later twentieth century, these have survived to give the room a remarkable atmosphere and a sense of accumulated history. Preserving the silk textiles in this room has been a slow task involving new research, much consultation and the employment of the latest conservation techniques. The following account charts the process of analysing and executing the conservation works.

When Castletown first opened to the public in 1967 the house was largely interpreted in terms of the eighteenth century, dominated by the creative spirits of Speaker Conolly, his wife Katherine, and subsequently by their nephew Tom and his wife Lady Louisa. In recent years an appreciation has developed that the architectural and decorative history of the house is more complicated. In the nineteenth century, Lady Louisa's great, great nephew Thomas Conolly (1823-1876) carried out extensive redecorations throughout the house in the years before his death in 1876, works which included the Red Drawing Room. Since work began in 2014 gathering material for Castletown's Conservation Management Plan, the rooms have been interpreted as multilayered survivors of the eighteenth, nineteenth and twentieth centuries, with their conservation forming part of their continuing history.[2] Alongside this inclusive approach towards the interpretation of the house, respect for surviving historic textiles and paint surfaces has increased, particularly in the Red Drawing Room, where current research and conserva-

1 – The Red Drawing Room photographed in 1961 (Irish Architectural Archive: Hugh Doran Collection)

tion works are concerned with preserving this grand, highly patinated interior.

Conceived almost certainly as a wainscoted common parlour in the 1720s, the Red Drawing Room is situated on the ground-floor north enfilade between the Green Drawing Room (or Saloon) and the Brown Study. Remains of the early panelled decoration probably survive hidden beneath the present scheme, although it has not yet been possible to investigate their nature, as was the case during the restoration of the adjoining Green Drawing Room in 1985.[3] The Red and the adjoining Green drawing rooms were radically altered by Tom and Lady Louisa Conolly in 1764-68, almost certainly influenced by works carried out at Leinster House for the Duke of Leinster.[4] As a result, the published designs of Serlio and the influence of the British architect Isaac Ware are evident in the ceilings, mahogany doors, carved doorcases and joinery supplied in lengths by Richard Cranfield, who was paid £223 1s 5d on the 14th September 1768.[5] In September of that year, the white Cararra chimney pieces in both rooms were brought over from London, possibly supplied by Deval & Son.[6] Both rooms were hung in silk damask; remains of the Green Drawing Room's pale-green Spitalfields silk were discovered during the 1985 restorations. Evidence of the Red Drawing Room's 1760s silk has not been found, but in August 1770 it was described by Lady Sophia, Countess of Shelburne as a 'damask of four colours'.[7] Much is still unknown about the late eighteenth-century furnishing of this drawing room. However, some of Tom and Lady Louisa's furnishings survive *in situ*, and between these, Lady Louisa's letters and the eighteenth-century items evident in the *c*.1880 and 1912 photographs and the 1894 inventory, the impression created is of an elegant room that was redolent of her aristocratic yet informal personality.

Both rooms were hung with new silk in the middle decades of the nineteenth century. No household accounts have been found to confirm this, but it is assumed that this work was carried out by Thomas Conolly (1823-1876) – hereafter referred to as Thomas Conolly II – between his marriage to Sarah Eliza Shaw (1846-1921) in 1868 and his death eight years later. The Green Drawing Room was hung in a plain dark-green silk, and the Red Drawing Room in a crimson hand-woven damask. In the 1893-94 inventory the green silk was described as 'much faded, old & torn in places'.[8] This silk was subsequently cut down to the level of the gilt fillets, and the walls were painted blue and then, after 1967, dark green. The Green Drawing Room was re-hung with new silk in 1985 in a restoration intended to return it to its 1768 appearance. This restoration was a highly symbolic act of triumph over adversity on the part of the Castletown Foundation, the then-owners of the house, as the original house contents had been recently secured for posterity through a public appeal. The additional generosity of donors and advisors made possible the return of one room to the decorative glamour of Lady Louisa's period.[9] While the Foundation's achievement remains, other conservation perspectives have inevitably developed since 1985, and these have formed the basis of the philosophy for the current conservation of the adjoining Red Drawing Room.

While the restrained architecture of the Red Drawing Room reflects the late eighteenth-century neoclassical taste of Lady Louisa, decoratively the room is dominated by

2 – The Red Drawing Room, c.1986
(courtesy Davison Photo)

the mid-nineteenth-century crimson silk. The paintwork of woodwork and ceilings has not been renewed for at least a century, and the large and dominant Aubusson carpet seems to date from the mid-Victorian redecoration. Since 1967 the Red Drawing Room has mainly contained furniture original to the house, although not necessarily to this room, and has featured a dense and a changeable picture-hang, including some original but also loaned and bought-in portraits and landscapes (Plate 2). The original furniture includes the carpet, the pier glasses and perhaps some of the Chinese Chippendale seat furniture, all of which were *in situ* in 1893-94. The two most iconic Castletown pieces – Mrs Conolly's painted cabinet and the large mahogany writing bureau – were, in 1893-94, respectively in the Long Gallery and a ground-floor corridor. Recently, two encoignures have been a notable repatriation. Made by Roger Vandercruse (known as 'La Croix'), the Parisian *ébéniste*, they were bought by Lady Caroline Fox for Lady Louisa in 1763.[10] They were sold by Christie's on 19th May 1966 and bought back for Castletown in 2014.[11] Amongst the pre-nineteenth-century items that are gone are the '4 white and gold Louis XV1 elbow chairs in same figured crimson silk' and the 'steel and brass Boule cabinet in ebony wood' that were listed in the 1893-94 inventory and can be seen in the *c.1880* photograph (Plate 3).[12]

    The survival of significant 1760s architectural fittings alongside 1870s decoration,

illustrate two different periods of the house's development and present difficult decisions
as to how best preserve and present this space in a meaningful way. This interpretive
conundrum is not peculiar to the Red Drawing Room, and as the Conservation
Management Plan develops it will attempt to address the complexities of history and the
visitor experience in all the public spaces. The deterioration of the Red Drawing Room's
textile wall-hangings due to light damage, fluctuating atmospheric conditions and less
than careful re-hanging of pictures over the decades, has been a matter of concern for
many years. Although appreciated for being redolent of the shabby grandeur for which
Castletown has been noted, the deteriorating condition of the silk was increasingly at
odds with the conserved appearance of the other rooms open to the public. In the 1893-
94 inventory, the room was described as having walls 'covered in crimson & white figured silk to match furniture and in good condition, one small tear to left of fireplace'.[13]
Images taken by Hugh Doran in 1961 (Plate 1), five years before the contents sale, show
huge picture canvases still *in situ*, but the silk around the chimney piece is deteriorated
and patched with what are presumed to be reused window curtains of the same material.
This deterioration continued once the house opened to the public, and between 1991 and
2005 five reports were commissioned from textile conservators in an attempt to address
the issue of decay.[14] Faced with these huge walls of extremely delicate and damaged material, the approach of the experts differed. Some recommended removal of the silk and
wet cleaning, while some recommended reusing silk from behind pictures to reinforce

areas of poor quality. Others recommended the application of adhesive panels from behind, and others proposed *in-situ* treatment with various forms of netting.

Financial constraints, urgent structural repairs and the difficulties of tackling environmental issues at Castletown prevented an active campaign of conservation within the Red Drawing Room until recent years. There was also considerable debate within the OPW and the Castletown Foundation not only about the correct conservation approach, but also ethical and aesthetic considerations of conservation versus replication. This debate touched on the fundamental question of what and how much was to be preserved and presented at Castletown. The damaged silk and old paintwork could either be seen to be distracting from the fine architecture and fittings or as important reminders of changing historical decorative fashions and the variable fortunes of the Conolly family. Ultimately there was agreement that the layers of history evident in this room must be preserved if possible. In 2006 and 2012, Ksynia Marko, a National Trust textile conservation advisor, was asked to assess the previous treatment proposals and to make suggestions for a practical way forward in both the medium and long term.[15] By 2012 the internal environment of the house had been controlled and a careful regime of household conservation in place. As part of the preparatory work for the Conservation Management Plan, the silk was considered not in isolation, but in relation to the furnishings within the drawing room, the north enfilade of adjoining spaces, and the developing overall philosophy of presentation and interpretation of the house.

In August 2012 Ksynia Marko identified the damage that exposure to light and environmental conditions had done to the silk (Plate 5). It had fractured across the warp, creating ragged splits, seams had split and shrunk, and it was all brittle and very dirty.[16] The north wall, hidden from light, was in the best condition; the south wall was in the most advanced state of decay. Subject to trials and further discussion, four possible approaches were proposed – full replication, full conservation, a holding treatment or partial treatment and replication, weighing up the pros and cons of each. These options were developed fur-

4 – The Red Drawing Room
photographed after the 1966
contents sale
(courtesy Irish Architectural Archive)

opposite

3 – The Red Drawing Room,
facing south-west, c.1880
(courtesy Chris Shaw)

5 – *Ksynia Marko discussing the potential treatment proposals, 2012*

6 – *Ksynia Marko and May Berkouwer working on the silk conservation of the west wall, 2015*

7 – *May Berkouwer working on the lower section join between drops 13-14 on the East Wall*

opposite

8, 9 – *The east wall drop 5 before and after conservation*

10 – *The silk damask design*

(photos 5, 6, 7: the author; photos 8, 9, 10: May Berkouwer)

ther in May 2015 when May Berkouwer, an independent textile conservator, assessed the project. Working on the basis of minor intervention, she proposed different treatments for each wall and its individual problems.[17] One of the concerns was that if some of the silk was conserved and some was replaced, they would not sit comfortably together. The garnering of experienced outside comment has been a feature of the project, and has included informal advice from a number of experts.[18] Although opinions varied, there was general appreciation for the faded beauty of the ensemble. A conservation trial on a section of the west wall of the drawing room was commissioned in November 2015, enabled by a legacy generously bequeathed to the Castletown Foundation by the late Professor Kevin Nowlan. Different treatment options were under consideration, and trials were needed to check technical issues relating to the varied condition of the silk damask. This innovative and highly technical work involved removing old repairs, gently vacuuming some and surface-cleaning other parts of the silk, supporting damaged fabric with silk crêpeline attached to the rear, humidifying and rejoining split silk, patching, netting and infilling lost areas (Plates 6-9). The results were deemed a success by the OPW and the Castletown Foundation, and in December the Foundation agreed to fund the remainder of the west wall as a memorial to Kevin B. Nowlan. In November 2015 board member Frances Bailey visited the Royal Apartments in the Pitti Palace in Florence and noticed the close similarity between the wall coverings there and those in the Red Drawing Room at Castletown. Penelope Jenkins subsequently made a

detailed comparative study of the Castletown silk with the green-coloured and similarly patterned material in the Salon Verde of the Pitti Palace in 2016. This had been supplied by Francesco Fullini in 1854/55 for the Dukes of Tuscany.[19] She also compared it to the crimson silk in the Sale delle Udienze in the Palazzo Reale, Genoa, dating from 1843 and bought from Bernardo Solei for the King of Sardinia. It has not yet been proven that the Castletown material is Italian, or indeed whether Tom Conolly II was influenced by the Palazzo Pitti Royal Apartments, which he visited with his wife Sarah Eliza on the 28th February 1871, spending a day looking at its treasures.[20]

As part of the ongoing research on the room, Richard Humphries (Humphries Weaving, Suffolk) was commissioned in September 2014 to determine the nature and quality of the 1870s silk, as well as options for replication (Plate 10). His report identified the silk as being of the highest quality, undoubtedly hand-woven on a Jacquard loom, using semi-tonal weave structures to create variety and surface shine. It was considered possible that it was intended to be a replica of Lady

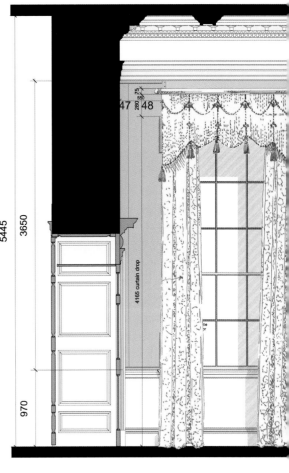

11 – Proposed curtains for the Red Drawing Room based on reconstructed evidence
(courtesy Sheehan + Barry Architects)

Louisa's 1760s original.[21] Nineteenth-century technical advances, however, allowed for tonal variations between the white and crimson silks, creating a four-colour effect. Despite the dirty and delicate condition of the silk, the report gave all involved in the project a heightened appreciation of the Victorian scheme. In May 2015 David Sheehan carried out a measured survey of the room and its silk hangings, which enabled plans to be developed for curtains, a potential picture-hang and the placement of furnishings.

In September 2015 Annabel Westman was commissioned to develop designs and specifications for new curtains. In February 2016 she also examined minutely the evidence in the room, the 1893-94 inventory, old photographs, as well as the fragmentary remains of nineteenth-century curtains surviving elsewhere in the house.[22] As a result she developed a template with David Sheehan for a fringed valance, trimmings and draw curtains (Plate 11). In March 2016 the OPW produced a statement of significance for the

room where the agreed approach for the conservation and holding treatments of the silk was set out.[23] This was in line with the Foundation's belief that all works at Castletown should be informed by historic research and that, if possible, all periods of history should be reflected in the presentation of the house. The west wall was substantially conserved by July 2017. As anticipated, the old silk is still recognisably patinated and faded in places, but it is no longer forlorn and ragged but cared for and 'held' for future years.

In the summer and autumn of 2017 the OPW funded the conservation of the east wall (Plates 12, 13), with that of the north planned for the spring of 2018. Upon the conservator's recommendations, the south wall will be treated rather differently.[24] As it is far more degraded and fragile, it will be cleaned, conserved where possible, patched and netted. Much thought was given to the possibility of replacing this wall with new fabric, but in the end the overall harmony of the room was considered most significant, and a holding process for the old silk agreed upon. In March 2017 the Apollo Foundation generously agreed to grant-aid the holding treatment for the south wall in 2018. Upon completion, it is hoped that the conservation works will enhance the visual harmony of the room, thus providing a more suitable backdrop to other decorative elements.

Parallel with the conservation works of the wall silk, a schedule of repair and conservation for other elements of the rooms was drawn up by Dr Dorothea Depner of the OPW and the Castletown Foundation. Although no redecoration is planned, a paint analysis survey will be commissioned to determine the chronology of colour schemes on woodwork and plasterwork, and to identify the presence or otherwise of any gilding. A key factor in the future success of the space is the need for curtains for the three windows. While a plain, suitably coloured fabric was a consideration, it was generally agreed that the most accurate option would be to reproduce the nineteenth-century silk to be made up as curtains as close as possible to the originals. Following Richard Humphries' 2014 analysis of the silk, his assistant Jenny Newman, using the best preserved fabric from the north wall and a tiny fragment from under the gilt fillet, drew up the intricate pattern. Colour assessments were initiated and samples were woven to compare modern weave quality, thread size and colours. Sets of samples were considered by the conservators, Annabel Westman, the OPW and the Castletown Foundation, resulting in further trials (Plate 14). In early 2017 the new fabric was commissioned, and delivered to Castletown in December. The tender for the curtains and trimmings was agreed, manufacturers approached, and with Annabel Westman as consultant, they will be commissioned and made in 2018. In 2016 the Foundation commissioned John Hart to repair and conserve the Chinese Chippendale furniture which has stood in the room for the past fifty years. The velvet plush upholstery was cleaned and conserved by early 2018, and six additional chairs from this suite will be re-covered in the newly woven reproduction damask.

Part of the conundrum facing the analysis of the Red Drawing Room is the incomplete surviving evidence relating to how it was furnished in the pre-Victorian era. References to decoration in Tom and Lady Louisa's household accounts and correspondence between the late 1750s and the 1780s have been quoted elsewhere; however, few can be related directly to the Red Drawing Room.[25] Neighbouring houses like Carton and Killadoon have inventories dating from the early nineteenth century which give a sense of how important rooms belonging to the Conolly relatives and neighbours appeared at the end of Tom and Louisa's lives. However, each of these houses has always differed significantly from Castletown, and parallels are only of a general kind.[26] The much later 1893-94 inventory at Castletown is the only detailed record known to survive of the contents, and in the Red Drawing Room (referred to as Crimson Drawing Room) it indicates a collection containing elements from the later eighteenth century through to the late nineteenth century. The Red Drawing Room contained up to eighteen mainly religious pictures. In addition, and surviving in the room today, were the eighteenth-century items mentioned above – the pier glasses now attributed to Richard Cranfield and James Jackson, the La Croix cabinets, and some of the Chippendale suite of seat furniture. The most striking original item still *in situ* is the huge Aubusson rug that appears to date from the 1870s. A 'Bombay' pair of console tables and suite of gilt seat furniture (now in Prehen, county Derry), a Boule cabinet, a large gilded centre table (subsequently in Carton and then Courtown House, county Kildare) and other items of seat furniture are no longer in the collection. Their arrangement may be seen in the *c*.1880 (Plate 3) and 1912 photos of the room (see p.103). With the exception of the recently acquired Lacroix cabinets, the original furnishings that survive today were purchased by Desmond Guinness before and during the 1966 contents sale, and acquired by the Castletown Foundation between 1985 and 1987.

The lack of Victorian furnishings in the collection today creates a historical imbalance in the room, but illustrates the post-1967 sympathy for the eighteenth-century interpretation of the house. With our new understanding of Tom Conolly II, the ambition now is to trace these items and, if available, return them for display. The most notable loss in the present collection are the eighteen pictures present in 1893-94. In 2013 Aidan O'Boyle was commissioned to report on the nature of the mid-nineteenth-century hang and its context in relation to other earlier Irish collections.[27] Significant pictures were identified both in this report and in subsequent consultations (see pp.98-107). While it is possible that some Red Drawing Room pictures had been collected by previous members of the Conolly family, those listed in 1893-94 appear to be a mid-nineteenth-century assembly by Tom Conolly II of religious paintings, dominated by large canvases hung in single file. There

12, 13 – The east wall before and after conservation 2017 (photos: May Berkouwer)

14– Annabel Westman assessing a woven sample in November 2015 (photo: the author)

were some significant pictures, including Murillo's *Christ after the Flagellation* (see p.104), bought from the collection of the exiled French King Louis-Philippe, a Vasari, *The Garden of Gethsemane*, previously in the collection of Louis Bonaparte, King of Holland, and a Holy Family after Correggio, attributed to Mazzolini.[28]

In 1875, the year before his death, Tom Conolly mortgaged Castletown for £98,000; in later years this caused his widow Eliza and his trustees considerable problems, resulting in a court order to sell chattels.[29] This, and the subsequent letting of the house, was presumably the reason for the 1893-94 inventory being drawn up. When the room was photographed for the *Georgian Society Records* in 1912 (see p.103), the picture-hang had been slightly altered as a result. Subsequently, there were sales of furniture and, perhaps, paintings to the Wills family (who rented the house from 1910), and in 1952 and 1957 at both Sotheby's and Christie's, so that by 1961 when the room was photographed by Hugh Doran some of the religious pictures had been replaced by large portraits (Plate 1). The remaining pictures were dispersed at the 1966 house sale held by Jackson-Stops & McCabe, and by Christie's in London.

In 2013, consultations with the National Gallery of Ireland as to how best to hang the room were held. One possibility was to hang a loan collection of religious paintings alongside reproductions of the most important originals in a manner similar to that described in the 1893-94 inventory. In August 2017 the OPW was generously offered a large loan collection of portraits, religious and classical subjects from the Schorr Collection. Previously on display in Hillsborough Castle, county Down, and in Birmingham City Art Gallery, these will form a denser hang of sacred and other subjects which will complement the architecture and the interior furnishings.

As the nineteenth-century appearance of the Red Drawing Room is more greatly understood and appreciated, its creation appears to be bound to the later life of Tom Conolly II. Lena Boylan wrote of how Conolly 'lived recklessly and exceeded the extravagances of his eighteenth-century namesake in his equipage and entertainments'.[30] No written evidence in his diaries and accounts has as yet been found as to the alterations that he seems to have affected to the house on his return from his travels in 1865. Tom's marriage to Eliza Shaw in 1868 (which brought a £10,000 settlement) and a series of land sales in the late 1860s may perhaps have been the incentive and facilitator for these works.[31] A recently discovered reference in *The Freeman's Journal* is perhaps significant:

> 5 April 1871 from our 'London Correspondent'. A London telegram says that one of the residences of Mr Thomas Conolly, MP, in the County Kildare, is to be taken for a royal residence, and that the Queen and the Prince of Wales will reside there during a portion of each year.[32]

If, indeed, this was the aspiration, and if Castletown was the residence in question, then it might explain and date the refurbishment works, which included the re-hanging of the Green and Red drawing rooms with new silk, the partial redecoration and reordering of the Long Gallery, and the creation of a library in what was formerly a ground-floor bedroom, now called the State Bedroom.[33] In 1871 a smoking room in the east wing was created for hunting parties, with dated chimney pieces. Related to this are seven architectural drawings still in the house of the unexecuted project for an elaborate Italianate new east wing, attributed to Frederick Darley.[34] Further research will hopefully clarify this mid-nineteenth-century renaissance of Castletown. The significant material found in recent years underlines the obligation not to obliterate evidence through insensitive conservation and restoration.

Generally this project has illuminated the importance of aged and conserved textiles in guiding the aesthetic appreciation of an historic interior. It is hoped that the conserved Red Drawing Room walls will offer an atmospheric context for the collections. The vision for the room has been the conservation of the wall silk, the creation of new curtains replicating those of the 1870s, the creation of an imaginative picture-hang that complements but hides the most damaged areas of silk, and the display of furniture that is both indigenous and relevant to the collection. Castletown is not only a symbol of the greatness of historic Irish decorative endeavours, it is also a survivor – of generations of one family and the vicissitudes of time. Exercising a lighter touch in terms of conservation and replication will allow the interior to remain 'a faded canvas', enabling imaginative visitor interaction.[35]

––––––

ACKNOWLEDGEMENTS

I would like to thank the members of the Castletown Foundation, the staff of the OPW, and May Berkouwer, Frank Lawrence, Simon Lincoln and Ksynia Marko for their help in the preparation of this article.

ENDNOTES

The following abbreviations are used:

IAA	Irish Architectural Archive
OPW	Office of Public Works
TCD	Trinity College Dublin

1   This project has been overseen by Mary Heffernan, OPW General Manager, and, since January 2016, co-ordinated by Dr Dorothea Depner.

2   The need for a single source of information which would inform decisions on the conservation and management at Castletown has been apparent for many years. Since 2014 a database of all relevant information has been compiled by the OPW, and within the house an architectural room by room assessment has been drawn up. In consultation with the Castletown Foundation, a framework for the plan has been developed which has been enormously influenced by those drawn up for the National Trust (NI). This carefully assesses the prevailing character and significance, history, conservation and presentation of each space. It is hoped that this project will be completed in the near future.

3   According to the Elton Hall plan, the chimney was situated on the west wall and this room was originally accessible from the west corridor. Howard Colvin and Maurice Craig (eds), *Architectural Drawings in the Library of Elton Hall by Sir John Vanbrugh and Sir Edward Lovett Pearce* (Oxford, 1964).

4   David Griffin, 'Castletown, Co. Kildare: the contribution of James, first Duke of Leinster', *Irish Architectural & Decorative Studies*, I, 1998, 120-45.

5   TCD, Conolly Papers, MS 3964, Personal account books of Thomas Conolly, 1767-1770, 24th September 1768.

6   David Griffin, 'Castletown, Co. Kildare'.

7   Bowood House Archives, Diary of Lady Sophia, Countess of Shelburne, 1st August 1770.

8   IAA, Castletown Papers J/11, Inventory 1893-94 (amended in 1898) of Castletown taken in conjunction with the resettlement of the Castletown estate.

9   Those who have helped Castletown were commemorated and acknowledged on donors boards erected by the Castletown Foundation and the OPW in the ground-floor east corridor in 2015 and 2017.

10 William Laffan, 'A Gift between Sisters', *Irish Arts Review*, no. 31, 2014, 152.

11 Thanks to the advice of John O'Connell, John Whitehead, and others.

12 The boulle cabinet was sold on 19th May 1966 by Christie's in London.

13 IAA, Castletown Papers, J/11, Inventory 1893-94 (amended in 1898) of Castletown.

14 The conservation proposals were made by Cliona Devitt, 1991; Historic Royal Palaces, 1995; Cliona Devitt and Cathy McClintock, 1997; Alexis Bernstorff, 2000; Dominique Rogers, 2005.

15 Ksynia Marko, 'Textile Conservation Advisory Report', unpublished report for OPW, 7th April 2006.

16 Ksynia Marko, 'Report of visit to review the options for the treatment of the 1870's red silk wall coverings lining the Red Drawing Room', unpublished report for the OPW (instigated by the Castletown Foundation), 17th August 2012.

17 May Berkower, 'Red Silk Damask Wall Coverings, Castletown, Co Kildare: assessment of condition and treatment options', unpublished report for OPW, June 2015. Both Ksynia Marko and May Berkower had worked on similar projects in the UK. In 1993 May had worked on the 1860s silk in the drawing room of the English Heritage-owned Brodsworth Hall, Derbyshire, and in 2001 Ksynia had conserved the 1830s damaged silk in the drawing room at Felbrig Hall, Norfolk, a property of the National Trust. Both rooms had problems of decaying silk, and in both properties the philosophy was to retain the damaged and faded material and to conserve *in situ*. Although not identical to Castletown, the success of these projects suggested that it might indeed be possible to save all of the silk wall coverings in the Red Drawing Room.

18 Those informally consulted included Julius Bryant, Keeper of Word & Image Dept, V&A Museum; Alec Cobbe, designer and artist; Christopher Gibbs, antiques dealer and historic adviser; John Goodall, architecture editor, *Country Life* magazine; John Harris, architectural historian; David Mlinaric, interior designer and former advisor to the National Trust; Jeremy Musson, architectural historian and author; Sean Rainbird, Director, National Gallery of Ireland. Alison Docherty generously gave her advice and experience gained from her conservation works at Hopetoun House, Edinburgh.

19 Penelope Jenkins, 'A Study of the Silk Wall-Coverings in the Red Drawing Room of Castletown House' (BA thesis), TCD, 2016. It has been noted that while similar, there are differences in scale between the pattern of the damask at Castletown and that at the Palazzo Pitti. Current research by the K.B. Nowlan Bursary recipient Laura McKenna promises to further elucidate the European exemplars for the Red Drawing Room and the motivation in emulating these royal audience chambers.

20 IAA, Accession No. 98/79, 1864-71, Diaries of Thomas Conolly (1823-76) 1870-71. I am indebted to Suzanne Pegley for this information.

21 Richard Humphries, 'Weaving Advisory Report: Castletown, Co Kildare: The Red Drawing Room', unpublished report for OPW, October 2014.

22 Annabel Westman, 'Red Drawing Room, Castletown House, Celbridge, Ireland: fabric and curtain design', unpublished report for OPW, 14th September 2015. Also 'Specification for making the three

crimson wool bullion pelmets with silk covered moulds and tassles for ornament' 28th September 2017 (unpublished) for OPW.

[23] In the statement prepared in association with Aisling Ní Bhriain of the OPW they outlined that they wished to conserve all surviving silk in the Red Drawing Room in Castletown, while acknowledging that methods adopted for each wall would need to respond to the condition of the silk. The conservation principles informing the works would include research and analysis, expert conservation advice, minimum intervention, reversibility where possible, repairing and preserving rather than replacing, and respecting earlier interventions of interest. The aim of intervention was not to achieve a perfect, seemingly flawless finish, but to reinstate the historic character to the room.

[24] Ksynia Marko, May Berkouwer 'Report of a visit to trial conservation treatment options for the 1870's red silk wall coverings in the Red Drawing Room with recommendations and estimates for further treatment', unpublished report for OPW, November 2015.

[25] David Griffin, 'Castletown, Co. Kildare'. See also Christopher Moore, 'Lady Louisa Conolly: mistress of Castletown 1759-1821', in J. Fenlon, N. Figgis and C. Marshall (eds), *New Perspectives: studies in art history in honour of Anne Crookshank* (Dublin, 1987) 123-41.

[26] The 1805 Killadoon inventory is the earliest surviving of seven in the possession of the Clements family and held at Killadoon, Co Kildare. The 1818 Carton inventory was purchased in 2015 by the Castletown Foundation and is held in the OPW-Maynooth University Archive and Research Centre at Castletown, MSPP/CAR/1.

[27] Aidan O'Boyle, 'A Report on the Arrangement of the Red Drawing Room at Castletown House', unpublished report for OPW, 2013. Further pictures were identified by members of the Castletown Foundation with generous assistance and advice from Alastair Laing.

[28] The Murillo painting hangs in Krannert Museum at the University of Illinois and the Vasari is now owned by the National Museum of Western Art, Tokyo; the whereabouts of the Mazzolini has not yet been established.

[29] I am indebted to Suzanne Pegley for providing this information from *The Nationalist and Leinster Times*, 3rd May 1890, which revealed that Conolly had mortgaged the entire Castletown estate for £98,000, which included lands in Donegal, Dublin and Kildare. Suzanne Pegley, 'Landscapes of Power: the social network of the power elite in mid-Victorian Ireland, case study of Thomas Conolly (1823-76) of Castletown, Co Kildare', unpublished PhD thesis, Maynooth University, 2017.

[30] Lena Boylan, 'The Conollys of Castletown', *Quarterly Bulletin of the Irish Georgian Society*, XI, no. 4, 1968, 44.

[31] Pegley, 'Landscapes of Power'.

[32] *The Freeman's Journal*, 5th April 1871. I am indebted to Suzanne Pegley and Frank Lawrence for this recently discovered information.

[33] Castletown almost certainly is the residence referred to, as Leixlip Castle, the other significant Conolly Kildare property, was let in the 1870s to Judge Edward C.S. Cole. John Colgan, *Leixlip, Co Kildare, Vol. 1* (Tyrconnell Press, Leixlip, 2005) 88. The proposal for a royal residence may have been intended to correct the absence of one in Ireland when compared with England, Scotland or the Isle of Wight.

[34] David Griffin, 'An Architectural History of Castletown', in Elizabeth Mayes (ed.), *Castletown, Decorative Arts* (OPW, Trim, 2011) 43.

[35] A useful guide to the philosophy behind the approach to the conservation of the room has been Margaret Ponsonby, 'Textiles and time: reactions to aged and conserved textiles in historic houses open to the public in England and the USA', *Journal of Textile History*, no. 42, 2011, 200-219.

———

Castletown in State ownership: reviving an Italianate palazzo, 1994-2017

DOROTHEA DEPNER

ASTLETOWN, IN THE WORDS OF THE LATE KEVIN B. NOWLAN, FORMER CHAIRMAN OF the Castletown Foundation, 'is a great Italian palace in the Liffey valley',[1] a description that deftly encapsulates the successful confluence of a distinct design and a particular locale. It acknowledges the international scale and significance of this neo-Palladian country house, which opens up to embrace the landscape and vistas towards the river and the Wicklow Mountains. Maintaining Castletown's integrity in this natural setting and preserving it for the enjoyment of current and future generations has been the task of the Office of Public Works (OPW) for the past twenty-four years. This article offers an overview of Castletown's revitalisation under OPW management since the house, a surrounding thirteen acres of land, and the Conolly Folly came into State ownership in 1994. It charts the major stages in the conservation of the house's interior, the restoration of its wings, designed landscape and farmyard, each step reinforcing the link between the house and its setting, enhancing our understanding of its history, and offering visitors an enjoyable experience.

When the Castletown Foundation transferred ownership of Castletown to the State in 1994, the building was in need of extensive repair. An OPW team, led by Kevin Conolly and John Cahill and comprising conservation architects, structural engineers and mechanical specialists, began the urgent work. In the first phase, external repairs to the roof, the parapet and the cornice of the main block were completed. The main block was covered with a protective temporary external roof that allowed the entire roof and parapet to be dismantled and repaired (Plate 1).[2] The original quarry in Edenderry was reopened in order to provide suitable replacement stone, 'hand-tooled to match the originals'.[3]

In parallel with the external repairs, non-destructive investigative works were

1 – Parapet removed and roof works in progress under protective roof

(photo: Frank Fennell Photography; courtesy Office of Public Works)

2 – Load-testing in the Long Gallery using bricks
(photo: Frank Fennell Photography)

3 – The Hunting Room in the east wing prior to restoration
(photo: Davison & Associates)

4 – The Hunting Room restored as an events venue, April 2012
(photo: Dara Mulhern)

(all photos courtesy OPW)

carried out, including load-testing the timber beams in the Long Gallery (Plate 2). The house contents – the majority of which are the property of the Castletown Foundation – were removed to environmentally stable storage facilities. The second phase of work involving ideal solutions for modern heating, power, emergency lighting, smoke detection and lift requirements began.[4] This service installation phase was completed in 1998. The third phase then followed, focusing on internal finishes in the main block and on installing a reheat kitchen, coffee shop and security room in the basement. The ceiling of the Long Gallery was strengthened and the plasterwork conserved before the house contents were returned.[5] The front and rear steps were removed, repaired and relaid, and the colonnades' plaster ceilings and west kitchen wing's roof were repaired. Castletown reopened to the public in 1999, but conservation continued (Plate 5).

Another extensive programme of works took place in 2006 and 2007. Careful paint analysis informed the selection of paint colours for the main house interiors, and lighting improvements, plaster and joinery repairs, and the conservation of the original mahogany handrails and doors, all contributed to 'the overall enhancement of the historic interior'.[6] The magnificent cantilevered staircase, which had been closed for a time, passed load-testing successfully in May 2007 and was subsequently reopened to the public.[7] Original timber panelling on the disused second floor was refreshed and the floors carefully repaired and cleaned to reveal their natural patina. This allowed a gallery to join this floor's OPW-Maynooth University Archive and Research Centre, launched by President Mary McAleese in 2008.[8] The Centre facilitates access to collections related to the history of Irish estates and holds several collections relating to Castletown and to other historic houses. During 2006-07, the kitchen wing also received considerable attention, with works revealing the unique character of the Old Kitchen, Housekeeper's Room and Ironing Room and incorporating an upgrade of the café and visitor services. Not surprisingly, this side of the house then became a magnet for visitors.

In 2009, craftsmen from Vetreria Artistica Galliano Ferro, a Venetian firm of historic glass-makers, came to Castletown to clean and restore the set of three Murano glass chandeliers in the Long Gallery. These date back to the 1770s and are unique in Ireland (Plate 6).[9] More recently, the Red Drawing Room's nineteenth-century silk wall-hangings and interiors were carefully conserved, a project realised in partnership with the Castletown Foundation and the Apollo Foundation, and discussed elsewhere in this volume by Christopher Moore (see pp.108-23). All these conservation projects were informed by research, and the current preparation of a conservation management plan will guide Castletown's management in years to come. Commending both the OPW's significant investment in preserving this historic site, and its staff's dedication, the Heritage Council awarded Castletown House full accreditation under its Museum Standards for Ireland Programme in 2012 and renewed its accreditation in 2016.[10]

Once the main block had been transformed into a safe museum environment and the kitchen wing converted into an attractive hub catering to visitors' needs, attention shifted to the former stable wing and east courtyard with the intention of restoring these

5 – View of Castletown's façade, June 2016
(photo: Will Pryce; courtesy COUNTRY LIFE Picture Library)

'for public use incidental to the house'.[11] The proposal submitted to Fáilte Ireland in 2008 by the OPW Architectural Services argued that the conversion of the stable wing would both create a unique venue in close proximity to the capital – one which broke the mould of 'the homogenous venues that are on offer' – and would contribute to 'the original concept of a demesne house … where the productivity of each element is important for the support of the house'.[12] The project's main purpose was to provide public access to the first floor of the stable wing and to connect this wing to the main house. With financial support of €3.5 million from Fáilte Ireland, the OPW's project team, led by Angela Rolfe and external consultants, transformed the stable wing within four years of securing matched funding. The new Events & Conference Centre was launched by the then Minister for Transport, Tourism & Sport, Leo Varadkar, just before Christmas 2011.

Castletown's vaulted stables, executed according to plans designed by Edward Lovett Pearce, are arranged on either side of the coach house and supported by Tuscan columns. As Patricia McCarthy points out in her essay 'Stables and Horses in Ireland c.1630-1840', they set a trend which Pearce's assistant, Richard Castle, continued in the stables he built at Carton and elsewhere in Ireland.[13] During restoration, the timber partitions, iron hayracks, mangers and iron fittings in the tack room were left *in situ* as a testament to the equestrian history of Castletown.[14] The coach house was returned to its previous form, its twentieth-century concrete floor was replaced with a limestone flagged floor, and the blocked-up arches were reopened and fitted with double-leaf doors.

The stable wing's two upper floors had been substantially destroyed in a fire in 1975 and had subsequently been converted into three domestic apartments. Only the long room on the first floor, fitted out in 1871 to accommodate a large library, had retained some of its distinct character (Plate 3).[15] A range of events now takes place under the

6 – The Long Gallery as featured in COUNTRY LIFE, *July 2016*

(photo: Will Pryce; courtesy COUNTRY LIFE Picture Library)

7 – East wing and courtyard prior to restoration, with light streaming through the 'magic door' in the colonnade, January 2007 (courtesy OPW)

8 – East wing and courtyard following restoration with new quadrant building, April 2012
(photo: Dara Mulhern; courtesy OPW)

9 – Pond dredged and silt removed to be used elsewhere in the demesne for planting
(photo by: Gretta Doyle; courtesy OPW)

Hunting Room's timber-boarded roof with its exposed trusses and ornate carvings (Plate 4). The original double height of the first-floor billiard room next to it was also restored. A lift, toilet facilities and a servery were installed to maximise the use of these spaces, and staff offices were added on the second floor.[16]

Unlike the link building behind the west colonnade, there had never been a physical connection between Castletown's stable wing and the central block. Instead, what the architects involved in the restoration referred to as a 'magic door' in the colonnade led directly into the east yard (Plate 7). Using materials that were sympathetic to the historic fabric, a new quadrant building was erected, linking the stable wing to the main house. It is just wide enough to accommodate a stairs and ramp, and narrow enough to be tucked within the depth of the existing annex building.[17] The east courtyard received an external surface of limestone setts, making it accessible for public use in all weather (Plate 8).

A look at Castletown's vibrant annual events programme will reveal that this part of the house is in use throughout the year for events and exhibitions, concerts and theatre performances, and it is the home to the popular monthly country and craft markets. As intended, the stable wing is today once again a productive element in its own right, adding to the overall sustainability of the country house setting.

Equally important to the remit of protecting the integrity of Castletown and enhancing the visitor experience has been the preservation of the historic setting, which was greatly helped by acquisitions of land that had formed part of the historic demesne. In 1997 the State acquired one hundred acres south of the house, and in 2001 the farmyard. In 2007 the OPW restored even greater integrity to the estate footprint by acquiring the former Coillte woods north and east of Castletown House, the Celbridge gate lodges, the Batty Langley Lodge and their surrounding lands. Of the 580 acres sold at auction in 1965,[18] by 2007 the State had slowly reassembled approximately 227 acres.

In tandem with the development of the Events and Conference Centre, and timed to coincide with the 300th anniversary of William Conolly's purchase of the Castletown estate in 1709, the OPW proposed a second major project under Fáilte Ireland's Capital Investment Programme, for which it received matched funding in 2011 – the restoration of the historic designed landscape and pathways between the house and the river Liffey.[19] Informed by research completed by Finola O'Kane and John Olley of University College Dublin,[20] a multidisciplinary team led by conservation architect Gretta Doyle – and including a civil construction engineer, a hydrology engineer, an ecologist, a hydrologist, the head gardener, a historic landscape consultant, and the estate manager – carried out an ambitious programme across the demesne to restore the historic parklands and pathways. In 2007 a new entrance from the motorway and a temporary car park were built at some distance east of the house, removing all traffic from the sensitive and scenic areas in front of, and around, the house. Over the course of the next six years, the OPW's garden and landscape conservation team restored Castletown's eighteenth-century landscape, which, as Finola O'Kane demonstrates in her book *Landscape Design in Eighteenth-Century Ireland*, owes much to Lady Louisa Conolly. Under her care, the emphasis shifted

*10, 11 – Batty Langley Lodge prior to conservation, December 2007
and after restoration, July 2016*
(photos: Davison & Associates; courtesy Irish Landmark Trust)

towards the river Liffey to the south and away from the woodlands and avenues north of the house that had been the focus of attention for the first two generations of Conollys at Castletown.[21] Lady Louisa's designed landscape included a network of paths around meadows and along waterways, with man-made accents carefully inserted into nature to create intimate, picturesque or downright dramatic settings – a classical temple here, a gothic lodge there, clusters of rare imported trees dotting wide open spaces, still ponds reflecting the house, gushing cascades and lively watercourses adding aural and visual effects.

A lot of this remarkable landscape had become overgrown or had disappeared from view entirely by 2007. In successive rounds of clearing, self-seeded trees and under-growth were removed, the historic vistas towards the Conolly Folly and the Wonderful Barn – both created by Katherine Conolly in the first half of the eighteenth century – were opened up again, the completely silted-up lower pond was dredged (Plate 9), a tree survey, ecological surveys, a geophysical survey and archaeological excavations were carried out (in the process of which a bronze age burial ground was discovered on the front lawn). Once vegetation had been cleared and historic features made visible, structures could be repaired and the original paths south of the house relaid in accordance with his-

toric maps. Even the gravel was carefully chosen to be as close as possible to the historic paths, visible in, for example, George Barrett's *View of Castletown* from *c*.1764. From 2012 onwards, the demesne features were tackled one by one: Mrs Siddons' Temple exudes elegance again, with its step base uncovered and its columns and cornice conserved. A mound of clay and grass now covers the ice house. The ruin of the bathing house was made safe. The gothic Batty Langley Lodge, conserved with financial support from the OPW, was turned into an enchanting holiday accommodation (Plates 10, 11).[22] The two cottages at the Celbridge gate were also conserved with financial support from OPW and they, too, are on long lease to the Irish Landmark Trust. The old stone bridges were repaired and additional wooden ones were made to straddle ha-has and watercourses in strategic places. The ha-ha walls, which function as crucial drainage throughout the estate, were also repaired, as was the dam at the end of the lower pond. Since the latter was refilled in early 2013, water has been rushing again down the restored cascade on its way to meet the Liffey (Plate 12). Visitors are now able to enjoy Castletown's parkland and the reciprocal views it affords. Data collected by people counters at various access points indicates the enduring popularity of Lady Louisa's designed landscape, with an average number of 50,000 people accessing the parkland each month in 2016. In July 2017 Castletown demesne received a Green Flag Award from An Taisce, as well as the Best Country House Park Pollinator Award in recognition of the sustainable and successful management of this wonderful natural resource.

12 – View of Castletown from the refilled pond
(photo: Alex Keys; courtesy Fáilte Ireland)

In 2016 a further element of the landscape was restored to the west and rear of the house – the former pleasure grounds. A survey drawing of Castletown from the 1850s, believed to be the work of Frederick Darley, clearly identifies the area behind the house as the pleasure grounds, and the area to the west – between the farmyard and west court-yard – as the flower garden (Plate 13). Evidence from the first (1837) and second (1870) edition Ordnance Survey maps and the 25" Ordnance Survey map (1899) shows that this part of the garden underwent considerable development in the nineteenth century when the walls and buildings that enclosed the garden were removed, although the linear flower beds and paths remained. Some time after 1840 and before 1870, a pond was created with an island to the west of the farmyard. By 1900 this pond had been extended to meet the area that formed the flower garden, erasing the clear distinction between pleasure grounds and flower garden, and signalling, it would seem, a transition to a more ornamental, less horticulturally demanding area. Archaeological exploration in 2012 revealed the infilled remains of a large oval water feature that corresponds to one included in the 1850s draw-ing by Darley. Other early garden features were probably levelled when a tennis court was installed in the western end of the garden in the 1940s/50s.[23] In the decades following the sale of the house in 1965, the area had become overgrown. It has now been restored as an enclosed flower garden offering a pleasurable retreat for visitors and an area for pri-

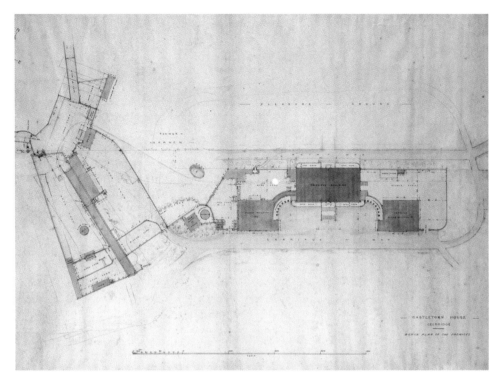

*13 – Frederick Darley (attrib.), plan of Castletown House
with pleasure grounds behind the house, c.1850s (photo: Davison & Associates)*

vate outdoor events (Plates 14, 15). Existing features such as a cypress grove and yew walk were incorporated into the design, and flower borders were planted against the western, eastern and south-eastern boundary fences. A path leads around the central lawn and to the cart gate into the farmyard.

This connection between the newly opened pleasure grounds and the farmyard has enabled the development of a new visitor experience distinct from touring the house or visiting the parklands. A key component in facilitating this new element is the restoration of the farmyard, which formed part of the original project proposal to Fáilte Ireland in 2008, together with the stable wing renovation and the landscape restoration, but did not receive funding. At the time, it was envisioned that the farmyard buildings could be converted, restored and refurbished to house a visitor orientation hub, plant centre, café, and home farm with some livestock. A new extension with public toilet facilities and a lift was proposed to allow universal access to all levels of the former cowshed, the largest farm building, including the top floor, which accommodates a room that measures almost 80m. Enabling works started in early 2009, and specialist contractors were hired for stone repairs, repointing and replastering, as well as roofing repairs to protect the integrity of the historic fabric. Phase two is ongoing and comprises the restoration and adaptation of the individual buildings and associated landscaping works.

14 – Pleasure grounds prior to restoration, January 2016
(photo: Liam Murphy)

15 – Pleasure grounds after completion, autumn 2016
(photo: Kevina Dunne)

16 – Upper paddock in the farmyard with view of the piggery and steam house, 2008
(photo: Davison & Associates; courtesy OPW)

opposite

17 – Upper paddock with restored piggery and steam house, July 2017
(photo: the author; courtesy OPW)

(all photos courtesy OPW)

Like the parkland, the home farm in Castletown was built to specifications from Lady Louisa Conolly in the 1780s to conform to her ideas of improved function and form. In a letter to her sister Emily, Duchess of Leinster, from 29th December 1787, Louisa joked that her delay in writing might be forgiven by sampling some of the produce from her recently built farm:

> ...when you come to eat some of the excellent pork, bacon, and ham that I hope our new piggery will afford, the good butter, cream and cheese that our new cow house (I hope) will produce, and the fine beef that our new bullock hovel will (I make no doubt) also furnish, I think that you will also pardon my neglect of writing, and allow that my time has been well-bestowed. Joking apart, we have engaged in a great deal of building of that sort which has required my constant attention, being the chief overseer, and having, as you know, great amusement in it. I am very proud of having made fifty cheeses this summer, which next year will nearly keep the family in that article, and my dairy is grown quite an object with me.[24]

A travel account written ten years later, in 1797, confirms this positive assessment of the home farm in Castletown and makes a point of referencing the productivity of one aspect as particularly noteworthy:

> Within these few years, Lady Louisa Conolly, wife to the present proprietor, and sister to the present Duke of Richmond, has erected a most spacious piggery, adjoining to the house, planned with the greatest neatness and convenience for the breed of that species of animal, containing several hundreds of beautifully-mottled and striped swine, of very curious colours.[25]

Since 2015 the carefully conserved piggery and adjacent smaller buildings in the upper paddock of the farmyard have been reopened to the public as a venue for children's art workshops over the summer months and, more recently, as the home of a visiting pet farm on summer weekends (Plates 16, 17). At present, the main farm building (the former cowshed) is being restored by the OPW team, and significant progress has been made to reintegrate this complex into the running of the demesne: service trenches have been dug and mechanical and electrical services installed, the cobbles conserved, windows inserted, doors repaired, and floors strengthened. In July 2017 two fully finished rooms at ground-floor level welcomed young visitors to the Big Brick Exhibition. It is hoped that once the remainder of the building is restored and accessible, it will serve as a resource that nurtures a playful, engaged encounter with Castletown's legacy and unique natural setting.

Of necessity, an overview of the work of over two decades condenses conservation and restoration projects into a few paragraphs and risks glossing over the vision, determination and sheer effort involved in realising their success, not to mention the countless smaller interventions that are part of the daily management of the site. All of these add to the way we can enjoy and experience Castletown today, and while the twenty-four years it has been in the ownership of the OPW account for little in Castletown's almost 300-year-long history, the long list of projects completed in the course of this short period is an achievement of which to be proud. In outlining the many steps that were involved, I hope that this article serves not just as an opportune reminder of these achievements, but also as a source of inspiration as we plan for Castletown's future. Just as importantly, I hope that it serves as testimony to the powerful connection that still exists today between the locale and the many individuals who have revitalised Castletown over this period, including the many staff, past and present, of the Office of Public Works.

———

ACKNOWLEDGEMENTS

A paper given at the 15th Annual Historic Houses Conference in June 2017 formed the basis of this article. I am greatly indebted to my colleagues in the OPW who have generously shared their knowledge and expertise with me, allowing me to chronicle projects that span more than two decades. In particular, I would like to thank Mary Heffernan, OPW, general manager of Castletown and the driving force behind all the restoration and development projects since 2006; Hugh Bonar, manager of Castletown, with an almost encyclopaedic knowledge of the OPW's National Historic Properties; Aisling Ní Bhriain, Greg Fagan, Gretta Doyle and Angela Rolfe in Architectural Services; the team (past and present) in Castletown, including Liam Murphy and Myles McKenna; and Christopher Moore and his fellow directors of the Castletown Foundation.

ENDNOTES

The following abbreviations are used: OPW   Office of Public Works

[1] Castletown House audio tour, script written by Tom Swift, produced by the Performance Corporation.

[2] Caroline Pegum, *Building for Government: the architecture of State Buildings, OPW, Ireland, 1900-2000* (Dublin, 1999) 147.

[3] John Cahill, 'Castletown House, Celbridge Co. Kildare', *Obair*, no. 8, 2002, 20-23: 21.

[4] *ibid.*, 22.

[5] Pegum, *Building for Government*, 148.

[6] Architectural Services, OPW, 'Event and Conference Centre, Visitor Orientation Hub, Liffey Walks and Water Features: Fáilte Ireland Funding Proposal', unpublished document, December 2008, 2.

[7] *ibid.*, 26. Also see White Young Green, 'Report on Load Testing of Cantilever Stone Stairs, Castletown House, Celbridge, Co. Kildare', September 2007.

[8] Architectural Services, OPW, 'Event and Conference Centre', 2, 26.

[9] Ann Keller, '"In Great Vogue": The Long Gallery of Castletown', in Elizabeth Mayes (ed.), *Castletown, Decorative Arts* (OPW, Trim, 2011) 57-65: 65.

[10] The Heritage Council, 'Museums Awarded for High Standards in Collections Care and Management', press release, 18th July 2016, <http://www.heritagecouncil.ie/news/news-features/museums-awarded-for-high-standards-in-collections-care-and-management>.

[11] Architectural Services, OPW, 'Event and Conference Centre', 9.

[12] *ibid.*, 21.

[13] Patricia McCarthy, 'Stables and Horses in Ireland *c*.1630-1840', *The Provost's House Stables: buildings and environs, Trinity College Dublin* (TRIARC, Dublin, 2008) 28-71: 39.

[14] *ibid.*, 47-51. See also Sarah Conolly-Carew, *The Children of Castletown House* (Dublin, 2015).

[15] David Griffin, 'An Architectural History of Castletown', in *Castletown, Decorative Arts*, 43.

[16] 'East Wing, Castletown House', *Obair*, 2012, 12-15:13f; Architectural Services, OPW. 'Event and Conference Centre', 15-19.

[17] *ibid.*, 14.

[18] 'Castletown House Sold by Auction', *The Irish Times*, 20th May 1965.

[19] The grant in question amounted to just over €1.5 million.

[20] Finola O'Kane, 'Castletown Landscape Report', unpublished report for the OPW, 2 vols, 1997; Finola O'Kane and John Olley, 'Designed Landscape Assessment of Castletown, Celbridge and Adjacent Demesnes for Kildare County Council', 2006; Finola O'Kane and John Olley, 'Submission of behalf of the OPW for the Local Area Plan for Castletown Demesne', 2007.

[21] Finola O'Kane, *Landscape Design in Eighteenth-Century Ireland: mixing foreign trees with the natives* (Cork, 2004) 59.

[22] For more information on the conservation of the Batty Langley Lodge, see Blackwood Associates, 'Batty Langley Lodge', *Architecture Ireland*, no. 253, 2010, 38-39.

[23] Melanie McQuade, 'Test Excavations Pleasure Gardens Castletown House, Celbridge, Co. Kildare', report for the OPW, 2012, 8f.

[24] Brian Fitzgerald (ed.), *Correspondence of Emily, Duchess of Leinster (1731-1814): Vol. III: Letters of Lady Louisa Conolly and William, Marquis of Kildare (2nd Duke of Leinster)*, (Dublin, 1957) 410.

[25] P.S., 'Tour in the Vicinity of Dublin Performed in the Autumn of 1797', *The Monthly Magazine*, 5 July 1798, 545-52, transcribed and edited by Rolf Loeber and Magda Stouthamer-Loeber, 'Dublin and its vicinity in 1797', *Irish Geography*, vol. 35, no. 2, 2002, 133-55: 150.

Lady Anne Conolly (1713-97): context and collection

NICOLA FIGGIS

Asearch for Edmond Garvey's views of Castletown in the Christie's sale catalogue of 1797 of Lady Anne Conolly's collection[1] piqued interest in this lesser known doyenne of Castletown House (Plates 1, 6). Eldest daughter of Thomas Wentworth (1672-1739), 1st Earl of Strafford, of Wentworth Castle, Yorkshire, she was to marry William James Conolly (1706-1754), nephew and heir of William 'Speaker' Conolly (1662-1729). On the death of Speaker Conolly, his widow Katherine (1660-1752) continued to live at Castletown, and it was not until she died in 1752 that William James and Lady Anne inherited Castletown, where they lived for a relatively short period, due to his untimely death two years later.

The attempt to delve further into Lady Anne's family history has proved somewhat challenging, with the repetition of family names over several generations. In addition, the succession of the earls of Strafford is acknowledged as particularly complicated, with the title being created three times in British history.[2] The aim of this short notice is therefore is to piece together preliminary research on Lady Anne and her family and to provide a brief overview of her collection, which was auctioned over two days, on 13th and 14th June 1797 by Christie's at No. 5 St James's Square, London.

Lady Anne's father Thomas Wentworth (1672-1739) was a grand-nephew of the more illustrious Sir Thomas Wentworth (1593-1641), 1st Earl of Strafford. In the late 1630s the latter was captured strikingly in armour by van Dyck in several portraits, after which numerous copies were produced (Plate 2) (including one at Castletown). A staunch royalist, and minister of Charles I, Lord Strafford served unpopularly in Ireland both as Lord Deputy in the 1630s and in 1640 as Lord Lieutenant of Ireland in the year before his execution. Fifty-five years later, in 1695, Thomas Wentworth inherited from his uncle William the baronetcy of Raby, another family title, but the estates were left instead to Thomas Watson, his aunt's nephew. However, as a reward for his own diplomatic efforts

1 – *Artist unknown (circle of Thomas Bardwell)*, LADY ANNE CONOLLY
date unknown, oil on canvas, 217 x 151 cm (Wrotham Park Collection; photo: Castletown Foundation)

Earl of Strafford.

2 – after Sir Anthony van Dyck, SIR THOMAS WENTWORTH, EARL OF STRAFFORD
c.1633, oil on canvas, 124.5 x 108 cm (National Portrait Gallery, London; on display at Lyme Park, Stockport)

as British Ambassador Extraordinary to The Hague, in 1711 Thomas Wentworth was elevated in the peerage as 1st Earl of Strafford of the second creation. To balance his lack of inherited funds, on 6th September 1711 Thomas Wentworth married Anne (d.1754), the heiress of Sir Henry Johnson of Bradenham, Buckinghamshire, a wealthy shipbuilder with estates in Suffolk and Bedfordshire. With new money from this Hogarthian marriage *à la mode*, the Earl and Countess shortly afterwards bought a prestigious London

3 – Gawen Hamilton, THOMAS WENTWORTH, EARL OF STRAFFORD, AND HIS FAMILY
c.1732, oil on canvas, 94 x 84 cm (private collection / Bridgeman Art Gallery)

residence at No. 5 St James's Square, dating to 1676, immediately adjacent to houses owned by the Earl of Portland and the Duke of Kent. As discussed at length by Hannah Greig, the newlyweds attempted to ensure their place in polite society.[3] The Countess set about equipping the house, their wealth and status emphasised by the inclusion of the family crest on many objects.[4] She had to haggle over the furnishings of the previous owner, Sir Richard Child, in respect of wall-glasses, marble tables, over-door pictures and the fittings of one room 'hung with Giult Leathere the Handsomest I ever see'.[5]

The couple subsequently had one son William (1722-1791) and three daughters; the eldest, Lady Anne, who was born on 5th March 1713, is the subject of this short notice. Like her mother, she became a devotee of fashionable life and attended court.[6] A group portrait by Gawen Hamilton painted in *c*.1732 (Plate 3) shows the Strafford family in a grand reception room, presumably at No. 5 St James's Square, with Thomas Wentworth resplendent on his gilded armchair, the top rail surmounted by an earl's coronet. While the devoted son and heir is the centre of attention, Lady Anne and her two sisters, albeit dressed in their finery and taking tea, are clearly relegated to one side.[7]

In 1739 Thomas Wentworth, the 1st Earl, died, and Lady Anne's brother William succeeded him as 2nd Earl of Strafford. He went on to make lavish changes to the house, including rebuilding to the designs of Matthew Brettingham in the late 1740s.[8] Among his circle, he could boast as a friend the art historian Horace Walpole, who, in his *Anecdotes of Painting*, recorded that a French painter, Clermont, had decorated Lord Strafford's 'eating room' with grotesque decoration, after Raphael's designs for the Vatican loggia.[9] One can assume that William would have consulted Walpole, an arbiter of eighteenth-century taste in Old Master paintings and author of *Aedes Walpolianae* (London, 1747, concerning Robert Walpole's collection at Houghton Hall), on any additions that he may have made to augment the Wentworth family picture collection.

William's sister, Lady Anne (Plates 1, 6), at the age of twenty, on 28th April 1733, married William James Conolly (1706-1754), MP for Ballyshannon, son of Speaker Conolly's only brother, Patrick. In 1731, two years earlier, William had purchased Leixlip Castle (Plate 4), which became their Irish home. William Conolly and Lady Anne had one son, Thomas (Tom) (1738-1803) and seven daughters, among them Frances, Anne, Harriet and Caroline. Lady Anne clearly wished to continue in the style to which she had become accustomed (Plate 5), and in October 1733 attended Dublin Castle. Clearly amused by the viceroy's wife, she wrote 'I like Queen Dorset much better than Queen Caroline'. In general, however, she was disdainful of what she perceived as the provincialism of Ireland, looking down in particular on country house architecture. According to Barnard, 'even Castletown barely passed muster'.[10] In June 1733, soon after his marriage to Lady Anne, William purchased Stretton Hall, Staffordshire, for £15,000, to give her an English home. In his own words, Stretton Hall was 'quite a half-way house ... to rest at [being] 130 miles from London [and] 136 miles from Holyhead'.[11]

Not until September 1752, on the death of Speaker Conolly's widow Katherine, did they move to Castletown House, but their residency there was to be short lived due to the untimely death of William Conolly in 1754. Lady Anne returned with her children to London, leasing rooms at No. 6 Grosvenor Square from 1755 until 1796, the year before her death. In this elegant house, with its grand entrance hall and stairway,[12] she had space to entertain friends in London society, such as Lady Mary Coke, and, like her, would have been a regular attender at court.[13]

In 1759, when Tom Conolly reached his majority, he inherited Castletown, along

4 – Joseph Tudor, VIEW OF LEIXLIP CASTLE WITH THE SALMON LEAP
c.1752, oil on plaster, 157.5 x 157.5 cm (detail)

5 – Manuscript bill to Lady Anne Conolly for fabrics
(both illus courtesy OPW / Castletown Foundation)

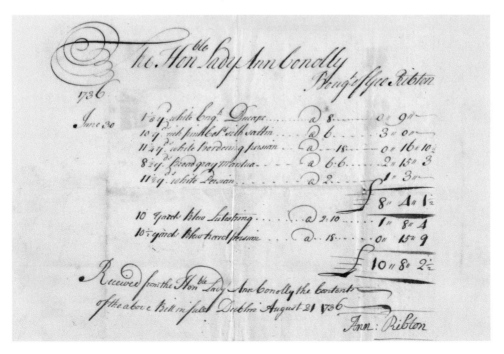

6 – Jean-Étienne Liotard
(1702-1789),
LADY ANNE CONOLLY
c.1754, pastel

7 – Anthony Van Dyck,
THOMAS WENTWORTH, EARL OF
CLEVELAND (1591-1667) WITH
HIS FIRST WIFE, ANNE, COUNTESS
OF CLEVELAND (D. 1638) AND
THEIR TWO CHILDREN
c.1636, oil on canvas, 156 x 246 cm

(both illus courtesy Wrotham Park
Collection)

with debts amounting to £36,000.[14] In the same year Tom married Lady Louisa Lennox, the Duchess of Leinster's sister. Far from being the marriage of convenience of his maternal grandfather, it was the match of neighbouring sweethearts. Between structural and decorative changes to the house which cost £25,000, and the expenses involved in running and maintaining his properties, including Leixlip Castle, Tom's annual income of £27,000 (in 1799) from estates in Ireland, was to prove inadequate.[15]

In 1791 Lady Anne's brother, William Wentworth, died childless, and his effects were left to her for her life, including the family property at No. 5 St James's Square. In spite of verbal promises to the cash-strapped Tom Conolly, whom the 2nd Earl had subsequently criticised for want of discipline, Strafford's last will stipulated that on Lady Anne's death, the effects should be passed to George Byng Junior (1764-1847) of Wrotham Park, Middlesex, Lady Anne's grandson.[16] Lady Anne was so outraged at her brother's will that she took legal proceedings in January 1792 to nullify it.[17] This seems to have had the effect of allowing her executors to sell the contents of the house, including the paintings, rather than passing them on directly to George Byng.

Over five years later, on 17th February 1797, Lady Anne herself died. After only four months, on 13th and 14th June 1797, a sale was held by Christie's at her 'late mansion' at St James's Square. The catalogue reveals that in scale this was a relatively modest collection of paintings for a London house compared with those of the long established Devonshire, Bedford, Northumberland and Spencer dynasties.[18] The portraits would appear to have descended through her family, such as the large family group by Anthony van Dyck (lot 38), showing Thomas Wentworth, Earl of Cleveland (1591-1667) with his first wife, Anne, Countess of Cleveland (d.1638) and their two children, Thomas, later 5th Lord Wentworth (1613-1665) and Anne (1623-1697) (Plate 7).[19] At the sale this portrait sold for £231, acquired by 'Byng', undoubtedly George Byng Jr, the future owner of the house, along with six other paintings of lesser value, including a half-length portrait by van Dyck of the 1st Earl of Strafford in armour (lot 34), and a full-length portrait of Queen Anne by Godfrey Kneller (lot 30a).

Also included in the same sale were several copies after portraits by van Dyck. Documents relating to a group of portraits commissioned by Thomas Wentworth (1593-1641) reveal that along with the original works, replicas by other artists could be ordered simultaneously. The rates recorded were £20 for a half-length and £30 for a full-length, an opportunity clearly availed of in Wentworth's case given the large number of copies which are known to exist after his portraits by van Dyck (National Portrait Gallery, London; Rockingham Castle, Northamptonshire; Euston Hall, Suffolk; Castletown House).[20]

Apart from family portraits by van Dyck and royal portraits by Peter Lely (lot 32) and Godfrey Kneller (lot 30a), Lady Anne Conolly's sale catalogue reflects the prevail-

ing taste of the eighteenth century for Italian mythological and religious pieces by artists like Guido Reni and Titian (lot 35), as well as seventeenth-century Dutch landscapes. It also serves as a reminder of the acceptability of collecting copies such as those included in the sale after Raphael, Veronese and Carlo Maratta. It is interesting to note that there is no work by any of the great British portraitists of the second half of the eighteenth century in the sale which William Wentworth or Lady Anne might have commissioned. The two views of Castletown by the Irish artist Edmund Garvey (lot 7) appear to have been commissioned by Tom Conolly as a gift for his uncle (as discussed by Jeanne Meldon, pp.156-60).

In addition to paintings and sculpture, which appear here in the Appendix, the catalogue also included 'verd antique slabs, large glasses, library of books, household furniture, &c.', indicating a major clearance of the house contents before the arrival of George Byng, who was forced to pay for anything from the sale that he wished to retain. One can only speculate on Tom Conolly's mild satisfaction at the price of the large van Dyck group portrait (Plate 7), as having sold at £231 it appears to have increased substantially in value. Lord Cleveland's Schedule of Debts includes '£100' owed to van Dyck, which was most likely for the same portrait.[21]

———

ACKNOWLEDGEMENTS

Grateful thanks are due to Jane Fenlon, Mary Heffernan, Christopher Moore, Charles Dace and Elizabeth Mayes, as well as to Jennifer Downey for generously sharing her research on the Conolly portraits. I am also indebted to Conor Lucey for suggesting useful sources and for his most helpful comments.

ENDNOTES

[1] Getty Provenance Index Databases, http://piprod.getty.edu/starweb/pi/servlet.starweb?path= pi/pi. web, accessed November 2017. Original catalogue at Christie Manson & Woods, London. Some editorial modifications have been made to the appended catalogue on pages 152-55 for clarity.

[2] Hannah Greig, T*he Beau Monde: fashionable society in Georgian London* (OUP, 2013) 271, n.8.

[3] This attempt was ultimately unsuccessful as in 1715 the Whigs attempted to have Thomas Wentworth impeached for apparent treachery with the French in the course of his diplomatic work on the unpopular Treaty of Utrecht. Greig, *Beau Monde*, 37-47.

[4] Greig, *Beau Monde*, 43.

[5] 'St. James's Square: No 5', in F.H.W. Sheppard (ed.), *Survey of London: Volumes 29 and 30, St James Westminster, Part 1* (London, 1960) 99-103. British History Online, http://www.british-history. ac.uk/survey-london/vols29-30/pt1/pp99-103, accessed 12th January 2018.

[6] In October 1733 Lady Anne visited her aunt, Anne Donelan, to give her a preview of her dress and jewels before being presented at court. Greig, *Beau Monde*, 119.

[7] As the eldest daughter, it is likely to be Lady Anne on the extreme right in charge of pouring the tea.

[8] 'St. James's Square: No 5' and British History Online (see note 5).

[9] *ibid.*

[10] For references to Dublin Castle, see Toby Barnard, *Making the Grand Figure: lives and possessions in Ireland, 1641-1770* (Yale, 2004) 3, 50. On 21st August 1736 she purchased silks and a 'Broad gray Mantua' gown from George Ribton in Dublin (Plate 5). In Elizabeth Mayes (ed.), *Castletown: Decorative Arts* (OPW, Trim, 2011) 226, cat. FC136, a facsimilie of the document appears on the verso of the dustjacket.

[11] A.P.W. Malcomson, 'The fall of the house of Conolly 1758-1803', in Allan Blackstock and Eoin Magennis (eds), *Politics and Political Culture in Britain and Ireland, 1750-1850: essays in tribute to Peter Jupp* (Belfast, 2007) 123.

[12] 'Grosvenor Square: Individual Houses built before 1926', in F.H.W Sheppard (ed.), *Survey of London: Volume 40, the Grosvenor Estate in Mayfair, Part 2, The Buildings,*(London, 1980) 117-66. British History Online http://www.british-history.ac.uk/survey-london/vol40/pt2/pp117-166 accessed 10th January 2018.

[13] Greig, *Beau Monde*, 198. In 1768, over dinner, they discussed the scandal that was brewing about her daughter-in-law's sister, Lady Sarah Bunbury, who was about to abscond with the father of her illegitimate child.

[14] James McGuire and James Quinn (eds), *Dictionary of Irish Biography: from the earliest times to the year 2002*, 9 vols (Cambridge, 2009) II, 774-75. These debts were incurred after the death of Speaker Conolly who was reputed to be the wealthiest man in Ireland in 1729, with an annual income amounting to £17,000, *Oxford Dictionary of National Biography*, www.oxforddnb.com.

[15] McGuire and Quinn (eds), *Dictionary of Irish Biography*, 775.

[16] Son of her daughter, Anne Byng (d.1806), married to George Byng Senior (b.1735).

[17] Malcomson, 'The fall of the house of Conolly', 123.

[18] See Giles Waterfield, 'The Town House as Gallery of Art', *London Journal*, vol. 20, no. 1, 1995, 47.

[19] See Susan J. Barnes et al, *Van Dyck, A Complete Catalogue of the Paintings* (Yale, 2004) 491-92. The provenance states that the portrait passed from William Wentworth to Anne Conolly.

[20] Oliver Millar, *Van Dyck in England* (National Portrait Gallery, London 1982) 69.

[21] Barnes et al., *Van Dyck*, fig. IV.78. On 21st October 1633, Lord Wentworth paid £40 for a full length portrait of Queen Henrietta Maria, *ibid.*, 524. The larger sum of £100 for a work painted in the same decade, is likely to indicate a group portrait.

———

APPENDIX

CHRISTIE'S SALE, London, 13th-14th June 1797   *overleaf*

APPENDIX

CHRISTIE'S SALE, London, 13th-14th June 1797
(reproduced courtesy of the Getty Provenance Index)

the following abbreviations are used:

		Slade	Thomas Moore Slade
Bessborough	Frederick Ponsonby,	Spackman	Charles Spackman
	3rd Earl of Bessborough	Strange	John Strange
Bryan	Michael Bryan	Smith	[?] Smith, Oxford Street
Christie	James Christie (II)	Vulliamy	Benjamin Lewis Vulliamy

lot	artist / title	sold (13.6.1797)	buyer
1	ANONYMOUS Two portraits, and flight into Egypt, small [paintings]	£0 19s	Seguier
2	ITALIAN SCHOOL *Orpheus playing on a violin* [painting]	£0 17s	Seguier
3	ANONYMOUS Two, a night scene, and one of fruit and still life [paintings]	£0 12s	Thwaites
4	VERELST (Dutch) Three, pictures of flowers, door pieces [paintings]	£2 2s	Seguier
5	ANONYMOUS Two views of Wentworth castle, and 2 three-quarter portraits [paintings]	£0 6s	Lewis
6	ANONYMOUS A portrait of Thomas Earl of Strafford in his robes, half length [painting]	£0 14s	Thwaites
7	GARVEY, EDMUND (British) Two views taken on Mr. Connolly's estate, in Ireland [paintings]	£3 10s	Ewen
8	MARATTI, CARLO (Italian), copy after Danae and Leda, a pair, after [paintings]	£2 6s	Price
9	VERONESE (PAOLO CALIARI) (Italian), copy after A pair, emblematical, after [paintings]	£2 5s	Seguier
10a	DOMENICHINO (DOMENICO ZAMPIERI) (Italian) Administering the sacrament to St. Jerome [painting]		
10b	ROCCA, MICHELE (PARMIGIANINO) (Italian) Descent from the Cross [painting]	£3 5s	Slade

11	ITALIAN SCHOOL A Madonna and child, and two Italian sea-ports [paintings]	£2 10s	Price
12	ANONYMOUS Two of school-masters with their pupils, and 2 flower pieces [paintings]	£1 18s	Thwaites
13[a]	ANONYMOUS A small picture of the portraits of Lord Strafford and Bishop Laud [painting]		
13[b]	ANONYMOUS A drawing of a boy's head, and 2 drawings of a bridge [drawings]	£4 0s	Bessborough
14	GIORDANO, LUCA (Italian) Two, representing the annunciation [paintings]	£3 3s	Slade
15	GIORDANO, LUCA (Italian) Two, subjects from Ovid [paintings]	£2 12s	Wood
16	ANONYMOUS A half-length portrait of Ann Campbell, Countess of Strafford [painting]	unknown	unknown
17	ANONYMOUS A pair of views of Wentworth Castle [paintings]	£0 10s	Strange
18	MOUCHERON (Dutch) An upright landscape [painting]	£12 1s	Byng
19	ITALIAN SCHOOL Diana with her nymphs reposing [painting]	£4 8s	Bryan
20	RENI, GUIDO (Italian) A Madonna and child, after, and a half length portrait of a lady [paintings]	£1 10s	Price
21	RAFFAELLO SANTI (Italian), copy after The Holy Family, a copy [painting]	£7 7s	Bryan
22	VERONESE (PAOLO CALIARI) (Italian) A pair of allegorical subjects [paintings]	£3 3s	Wood
23	KNELLER, GODFREY, BART. (British) A whole-length portrait of Lady Strafford [painting]	£1 5s	Spackman
24	VELDE, WILLEM VAN DE (Dutch) A sea storm, with shipwreck [painting]	£2 2s	Thwaites

lot	artist / title	sold (13.6.1797)	buyer
25	DYCK, ANTHONIE VAN (Flemish), copy after A three-quarter portrait of Lord Strafford, after [painting]	£9 9s	Bryan
26	BASSANO (Italian) A large picture of the Creation [painting]	£2 12s	Wood
27	RENI, GUIDO (Italian), copy after David, with the head of Goliath, after [painting]	£2 14s	Wood
28	CARRACCI (Italian), copy after The Descent from the Cross, after the capital picture in the Orleans collection [painting]	£5 15s	Christie
29	ANONYMOUS Two portraits, three-quarters, brothers of Lord Strafford [paintings]	£0 10s	Strange
30	ANONYMOUS Two ditto [portraits], a young lady and gentleman [paintings]	£3 13s	Byng
30[a]	KNELLER, GODFREY, BART. (British) A whole-length portrait of Queen Anne [painting]	£1 1s	Byng
31	KNELLER, GODFREY, BART. (British) Two portraits of ladies, 3-quarters [paintings]	£0 15s	Jolley
32	LELY, PETER (British) Two ditto [portraits], King Charles the Second, and King James [paintings]	£1 1s	Jolley or Spackman
33	LELY, PETER (British) Two, a 3-quarter of Lady Apsley, and half-length of a lady at a fountain [paintings]	£1 3s	Breadan
34	DYCK, ANTHONIE VAN (Flemish) Half-length portrait of Thomas Earl of Strafford in armour [painting]	£25 4s	Byng
35	TIZIANO VECELLIO (Italian) Ditto [half-length] of a knight of the Golden Fleece [painting]	£22 1s	Byng
36	WALKER, ROBERT (British) A three-quarter portrait of Oliver Cromwell [painting]	£12 1s	Byng
37	MARATTI, CARLO (Italian) A large picture representing the Judgement of Paris [painting]	£4 4s	Price

38	DYCK, ANTHONIE VAN (Flemish) A remarkable and very capital family piece of Thomas Wentworth, Earl of Cleveland, with his lady, son, and daughter. -- Ever esteemed one of the finest pictures painted by this celebrated artist [painting] (Plate 7)	£231 0s	Byng
39	ANONYMOUS, copy after Five basso relievos, in imitation of the antique [sculptures]	£1 8s	Price
40	no entry		
41[a]	ANONYMOUS Four small bronzes, various figures, one of a dragon [sculptures]		
41[b]	ANONYMOUS 2 small heads, profiles in wax [sculptures]	£3 3s	Smith
42	ANONYMOUS A large bronze of the Venus de Medici, and one of the piper, large and capital, on pedestals [sculptures]	£5 15	Heath
43[a]	ANONYMOUS Three statues, and 6 sphinxes [sculptures]		
43[b]	ANONYMOUS 2 small figures plain [sculptures]	£0 7s	Bucking- hamshire
44	COOPER, SAMUEL (British) A fine miniature portrait of Oliver Cromwell [miniature]	—	bought in
45	VERONESE (PAOLO CALIARI) (Italian) Jupiter and Europa [painting]	£4 14s	bought in
46	LELY, PETER (British) Lady Sutherland [painting]	£2 12s	Toode
47	LELY, PETER (British) Lord Arlington [painting]	£1 16s	Smith
48	DYCK, ANTHONIE VAN (Flemish) King Charles II [painting]	—	bought in
49	PACE, MICHELANGELO (MICHELANGELO DA CAMPIDOGLIO) (Italian) A fruit piece, very capital [painting]	£6 6s	bought in
50	ANONYMOUS A statue of Henry the Eighth [sculpture]	£6 16s	Vulliamy

———

The lost landscapes of Castletown: a note on Edmund Garvey's views of Castletown

JEANNE MELDON

On the walls of the Green Drawing Room at Castletown hangs a painting by the Irish landscape painter Edmund Garvey, *A view of the River Liffey with the ruined tower of St Wolstan's Abbey, Celbridge, on the left bank and figures on the right*. On 22nd May 1784, Garvey wrote to Tom Conolly concerning four views of Castletown that he had recently completed:

> Sir
>
> I beg leave to inform you, the four views of Castletown are finish'd. The Earl of Strafford did me the great honor to come to see them and also Lady Ann Conolly. They (with great condescension) were so good as to approve of and seem much pleas'd with them. Notwithstanding I should wish to submit them to your and Lady Louisa Conolly's well known accurate judgement. I beg'd of my Lord to leave them a few days to show some Gentlemen I had the honor to be employ'd by you. My Lord seem'd anxious to know whether you intend to send them to him framed, I made bold to say I believ'd you did, and have had very neat frames for them, which dont come to 5 Gs each, if you should not approve of them, I have other pictures they will fit.
>
> I am with great respect Sir most humble most obedient
>
> Edm Garvey
> 22 May 1784
>
> I beg to know your commands how the other two are to be disposed of.[1]

1 – Edmund Garvey, A VIEW OF THE RIVER LIFFEY WITH THE RUINED TOWER OF ST WOLSTAN'S ABBEY...
1780s, oil on canvas, 91.5 x 135 cm (detail; full image overleaf)

Born in Kilkenny in 1738 or 1740, Edmund Garvey studied painting under Robert Carver in Dublin. He then spent much of his working life abroad, studying in Italy before settling in England.[2] Moving from Bath to London in 1777 probably brought Garvey into circles where he could have come into contact with Tom and Louisa Conolly. Commissioning such a series of demesne portraits was popular at the time, and Jonathan Fisher had completed a similar series of Belvoir Castle, county Down, in the 1760s. Thomas Roberts completed his pre-eminent series of Carton and Lucan demesnes in the 1770s. The letter's discussion as to whether Conolly intended 'to send them to [the lord] framed' indicates that he intended two of the paintings for his uncle, William Wentworth, the Earl of Strafford the 'Lord' mentioned in the letter.[3] Garvey's query as to 'how the other two were to be dispos'd' suggests that the four views were never intended to be hung together and that some may have been copies.

In February 1797 Tom Conolly's mother, Lady Anne Conolly (née Wentworth) died. Her effects were auctioned on 13th June 1797 by Christie's in London. Among them were 'two views taken on Mr Connolly's estate' sold to a Mr. Ewen.[4] Lady Anne Conolly had moved back to England when her husband, the Speaker's nephew William Conolly II, died in 1754. She bequeathed two views of Castletown to her daughter-in-law, Lady Louisa Conolly, in her will, and these two were probably sent to Ireland in the aftermath of her death.[5] The painting described in Castletown's 1893-94 inventory as 'Large Landscape River and Woodland scene with a tower rising to left, figure on right bank'[6] is probably one of them. No other inventory entry seems to relate to any of Garvey's other views. It still hangs at Castletown, forming part of the Castletown Foundation's collection. The Foundation bought it from Desmond Guinness in 1984, who had in turn purchased it privately from Lord Carew in 1966.

Lady Anne Conolly was by some accounts a 'strong-willed, volatile, meddlesome, domineering woman'.[7] As one of Thomas Conolly's guardians during his minority and a trustee of her husband's will, she had some control over the family estate until all her

2 – St Wostan's Abbey
(photo: the author)

opposite

3 – Edmund Garvey, A VIEW OF THE RIVER LIFFEY WITH THE RUINED TOWER OF ST WOLSTAN'S ABBEY, CELBRIDGE, ON THE LEFT BANK AND FIGURES ON THE RIGHT 1780s, oil on canvas, 91.5 x 135 cm (photo by David Davison; courtesy Castletown Foundation)

daughters were married in the 1770s. She and Tom Conolly were on good terms until around 1795, when various lawsuits and misunderstandings to do with land settlements began to embitter their relationship. They also soured Tom Conolly's relationship with his sisters for the remaining period of his life. Family estrangement intensified when the contents of Lady Anne's will were made known to her children.[8] Why did Lady Anne leave the views to Louisa and not to Tom? Her son, despite censorious correspondence from his uncle regarding his gambling habits and inability to save money, expected a substantial inheritance from Strafford, which if forthcoming would have alleviated his financial affairs. A picture of Wentworth Castle, received from the earl, hung in his dressing room at Castletown,[9] suggesting that the two paintings by Garvey may have been a reciprocal gift from Tom Conolly to his uncle. Despite this, his efforts to win favour with his uncle were spectacularly unsuccessful: he received £300 rather than the £3,000 he had been expecting.[10] It seems likely that Lady Anne bequeathed the two Grosvenor Square Garveys to Louisa, and that the two she had inherited from her brother, the Earl of Strafford, were sold at auction. Of the four views of Castletown, three are now lost.

John Warren, the Irish portraitist, praised Garvey 'for truth, colour, and Effect', finding 'his Aerial perspective' to be 'remarkably good & his Effects natural and Simple'. He could paint water and rocks 'mighty well' but his trees were 'rather rude and unfinish'd', and generally he was 'rather negligent in his execution' with his 'foregrounds often too heavy in Colour'. As a painter he had a 'great deal of merit' while his 'faults may be call'd those of a Genius', an assessment that appears more than a little glowing.[11] The one remaining Castletown view is of the riverside Liffey walk near the cottage ground, looking across to the ruins of St Wolstan's Abbey. There are accounts and map extracts detailing the purchase of the cottage ground (formerly belonging to St Wolstan's, although on the northern bank) and the purchase of land in Parsonstown in the 1770s.[12] The Castletown view displays some of the characteristics referred to in Warren's letter, particularly in respect of the foregound's water and rocks. Garvey clearly made some effort to distinguish the trees by species on the left river bank, although the dog/foal beside the figure on the right-hand river bank is less than convincing. The tree-planting depicted is consistent with eighteenth-century maps and surveys. Discovering the three lost views would contribute to the understanding and conservation of Castletown's eighteenth-century landscape design.

———

ACKNOWLEDGEMENTS

I am very grateful to the editor and referees for their constructive comments on an earlier draft. I would also like to acknowledge the very helpful staff at the Irish Architectural Archive.

ENDNOTES

[1]   National Library of Ireland, Conolly Papers, MS 41,341/9/1. See also Patrick Walsh and A.P.W. Malcomson, *The Conolly Archive* (Dublin, 2010) 326.

[2]   A. Crookshank and the Knight of Glin, *Ireland's Painters, 1600-1940* (Yale, 2002). The authors make no reference to the Castletown paintings. See also Nicola Figgis (ed.), *Art and Architecture of Ireland, Volume II: Painting 1600-1900* (Royal Irish Academy and Yale, 2015) 271-72.

[3]   Had the paintings been given to the Earl of Strafford in 1784, they would then have passed to the earl's sister, Anne, after his death in 1791 under the terms of the earl's will. See A.P.W. Malcomson, 'The fall of the house of Conolly 1758-1803', in Allan Blackstock and Eoin Magennis (eds), *Politics and Political Culture in Britain and Ireland, 1750-1850: essays in tribute to Peter Jupp* (Belfast, 2007) 107-156: 125.

[4]   I am grateful to Nicola Figgis for this information. See also Figgis (ed.), *Painting 1600-1900*, 272.

[5]   Public Record Office, National Archives, Kew, Probate 11/1286, 'I give and bequeath to my daughter-in-law the picture of the said Thomas Conolly and the two views of Castletown in Ireland which are in my house in Grosvenor Square in London.'

[6]   Irish Architectural Archive, Castletown Papers, J/11, Inventory 1893-94 (amended in 1898) of Castletown, 203; see also Elizabeth Mayes, *Castletown, Decorative Arts* (OPW, Trim, 2011) 126.

[7]   Malcomson, *The Fall of the House of Conolly*, 111.

[8]   *ibid.*, 107-56

[9]   *ibid.*, 125.

[10]   *ibid.*

[11]   P. McEvansoneya, 'An Irish artist goes to Bath: letters from John Warren to Andrew Caldwell, 1776-1784', *Irish Architectural and Decorative Studies*, II, 1999, 156 and 161-62.

[12]   Irish Architectural Archive, Castletown papers, E/13/1-8, Deeds relating to St Wolstan's, Celbridge, and Parsonstown Leixlip, 1706-1773.

———